2ND EDITION

A GUIDE TO
Essential
Human
Services

FREDERIC G. REAMER

NASW PRESS

National Association of Social Workers
Washington, DC

James J. Kelly, PhD, ACSW, LCSW, President
Elizabeth J. Clark, PhD, ACSW, MPH, Executive Director

Cheryl Y. Bradley, *Publisher*
Lisa M. O'Hearn, *Managing Editor*
Sarah Lowman, *Project Manager and Copyeditor*
Wayson R. Jones, *Proofreader*

Cover by Naylor Design, Inc.
Interior design by Electronic Quill Publishing Services
Printed and bound by Victor Graphics, Inc.

Library of Congress Cataloging-in-Publication Data

Reamer, Frederic G., 1953–
  A guide to essential human services / Frederic G. Reamer. — 2nd ed.
    p.   cm.
  ISBN 978-0-87101-397-2
  1. Human services—United States—Handbooks, manuals, etc. I. Title.
  HV91.R383 2010
  361.973—dc22

                                                    2010003501

Printed in the United States of America

For Deborah, Emma, and Leah

TABLE OF CONTENTS

PROVIDING INFORMATION AND REFERRALS TO PEOPLE IN NEED: AN INTRODUCTION

WE ALL NEED HELP from time to time. A sudden crisis, such as a tragic automobile accident or a health emergency, can turn our settled world upside down. Within minutes we may move from feeling carefree to feeling overwhelmed. Amid the blur of frantic telephone calls, family meetings, and consultations with professionals, we need to locate emergency resources and find emotional support. Other needs may emerge more slowly and with forewarning: An elderly parent may begin to show subtle signs of dementia; a toddler may begin to manifest signs of a developmental disability; a marriage may begin to show symptoms of stress.

On any given day, diverse groups of professionals, volunteers, and consumers need to locate helpful information and connect people in need with resources and services. Accomplishing this task is no easy matter. The human services field is wide and deep. Well-known and visible services include those provided by hospitals, community mental health centers, and nursing homes. Other services, such as those offered by furniture banks, crisis centers or hotlines for gay or lesbian adolescents, and emergency legal services for political refugees and immigrants, may be relatively invisible and hard to locate.

The primary purpose of A Guide to Essential Human Services is to help professionals, volunteers, and consumers locate helpful information and resources. The guide is divided into several sections. This introduction presents a brief overview of human services and ways to think about locating information and resources. My goal is to ensure that readers understand the full range of information and resources available to people in need and the factors to consider when assisting people in need.

Following the introduction, the guide presents a comprehensive overview of the diverse resources that are available in the United States for people in need. The guide is divided into sections that reflect major categories of needs that may arise during a person's life. These categories relate to specific problems (such as hunger, homelessness, unemployment, substance abuse, and mental illness), challenging time periods (such as adolescence and retirement), and special populations (such as veterans and victims of child abuse or domestic violence). As reflected in the sections, important areas of need are

- income
- housing
- food
- clothing
- energy
- transportation
- health care
- mental health
- addictions
- sexual orientation
- family life education
- children and adolescents
- abuse and neglect, including protective services
- military personnel and veterans
- immigrants and refugees
- education and literacy
- employment assistance
- aging and retirement, including financial and legal issues
- legal services and dispute resolution.

The Diversity of Human Need

People in need require information and resources in a variety of circumstances. Consider the following real-life examples:

- Olivia and Donald had been married for about six years. Donald had a serious alcohol problem and sometimes physically beat Olivia and their two young children when he became angry. Olivia was afraid that she and the children would be hurt by Donald during one of his tirades.

  Following an argument one evening, Olivia decided to leave Donald. In the middle of the night, Olivia quickly packed clothes, woke the children, and sneaked out of the house. Olivia and the children spent the night with a family friend. Olivia remembered a social worker at the local hospital who had once been helpful to her during a hospital stay. The next morning, Olivia telephoned the social worker and asked for advice about where she and the children might go for emergency help with shelter, food, money, and other needs.

- Pedro and Maria had recently immigrated to the United States from the Dominican Republic. The couple had great difficulty reading and speaking English and had a hard time finding affordable housing and employment. They were living temporarily with a cousin, who referred Pedro and Maria to her minister for advice about housing options, employment, and a variety of legal issues related to their immigration. The minister had difficulty communicating with the couple in Spanish and knew little about specific social and legal services available to recent immigrants.

- Alma, age 78, and Harris, age 81, had been married for nearly 54 years when Alma began showing symptoms of dementia. Two years later, Harris was finding it more and more difficult to care for his wife. According to Harris, Alma was becoming increasingly disoriented, agitated, and hard to manage.

  Larry, their son, was very concerned about his parents and, in particular, his father's ability to care for Alma. Larry was eager to find out whether any local agencies could provide his parents with home-based services to enable them to continue living together in their apartment.

- Sandra, the owner of a local convenience store, noticed that a relatively new customer often spoke to himself in a loud voice while he wandered around the store. Sandra tried to engage the man in con-versation, but the man ignored Sandra and continued to mutter to himself. The man was very disheveled and unshaven, and he reeked of body odor.

Sandra shared her concerns with a police officer who patrolled the neighborhood and occasionally came into the store. The police officer interviewed the man and quickly determined that he had been discharged recently from the psychiatric unit of a local hospi-tal. The police officer was eager to contact mental health profession-als who would be in a position to help the man.

Human Services: An Overview

Many different kinds of organizations provide human services for people in need. Some services are provided directly by government (public-sec-tor) agencies. At the federal level, for example, the U.S. Department of Housing and Urban Development (HUD) sponsors a variety of hous-ing assistance programs for low- and moderate-income people; the U.S. Department of Justice (DOJ) sponsors programs for at-risk adolescents and people on probation who struggle with substance abuse; and the U.S. Department of Health and Human Services (HHS) sponsors a number of programs for people who struggle with poverty, domestic violence, and mental illness.

Every state also has human services departments that sponsor pro-grams. The specific names of the departments vary, but every state has a child welfare department, a mental health department, and departments that provide services to elders who have difficulty caring for themselves, people who are deaf or blind, and people who are very ill and have no health insurance.

Many cities and towns also sponsor human services programs. For example, some cities sponsor after-school recreation programs for chil-dren, health clinics for low-income residents, and emergency assistance for domestic violence victims.

Many additional human services programs operate in the private sector, often through nonprofit agencies, such as community action programs, community mental health centers, family service agencies, emergency shelters, legal aid offices, home health care programs, and furniture banks. Some private-sector programs are run by for-profit organizations. Examples include for-profit agencies that operate nursing homes and rehabilitation clinics, substance abuse treatment programs, psychiatric facilities, and employee assistance programs.

Human services programs obtain funding from various sources. Many programs receive all or part of their funding from federal, state, and local government agencies. For example, the federal Department of Education may provide funding for special education programs, a state child welfare agency may fund foster care services, and a local city or town may fund summer recreation programs. Federal, state, and local government agencies often will contract with private agencies to deliver human services. Also, federal agencies may fund programs indirectly through state and local government agencies, and state agencies may fund programs administered by local public agencies.

Many private-sector programs rely on a combination of funding sources, including government agency funds, United Way or other federation grants, insurance fees, foundation grants, and client fees. For example, a shelter for victims of domestic violence may obtain funds from multiple sources, including a foundation grant, a United Way allocation, and a contract with a state or local public agency or women's commission.

Human services provided by public-sector and private-sector agencies take many forms. Some services are provided in residential settings, such as nursing homes, rehabilitation facilities, emergency shelters, foster and group homes, substance abuse treatment programs, and psychiatric hospitals. Many services are provided in so-called outpatient settings, such as family service agencies, community mental health centers, soup kitchens, government agency offices, lawyers' offices, courts, and private counseling offices. Increasingly, human services such as respite care, family intervention, hospice services, and home health care are provided in consumers' homes.

Many different types of personnel provide human services. Many service providers have formal education and training in one of the human services professions. The most prominent human services professions are

- social work
- psychology
- psychiatry
- marriage and family counseling
- counseling
- rehabilitation
- psychiatric nursing.

Other service providers have formal education and training in a field other than human services. For example, lawyers employed by a legal aid clinic may provide legal assistance to low-income people, and clergy may provide important supportive counseling. Many agencies also recruit and train volunteers to provide an impressive array of human services.

Providing Information and Referrals

Professionals and volunteers who are in a position to help people in need can use this pocket guide to acquaint themselves and consumers with the range of available information and resources. This guide provides a broad overview of the types of information and services available in many communities.

Professionals and volunteers who are advising people in need should consider four important questions:

1. What information, resources, and services do the individual or family need? People sometimes need
   - concrete resources, such as money, food, clothing, furniture, heat, transportation, emergency shelter, affordable housing, residential treatment, nursing home care, and employment;
   - supportive services, such as health care, homemaker services, respite care, foster care, adoption services, protective services, tutoring, literacy services, recreational services, financial planning, translation, interpreter services, and employment advice;
   - emotional support, such as crisis intervention, individual counseling, couples counseling, family counseling, group counseling, mediation, and mentoring;

- information about various topics, such as health benefits, family and medical leave, welfare benefits, parenting, legal, health, insurance, employment, addiction, and sex education.

2. What information can you collect about the people who are asking for help or who are in need? Professionals and volunteers should gather as much relevant information as possible about consumers' backgrounds and current circumstances. Typical assessment information involves

   - historical information, including family and relationship history, medical history, psychological history, educational history, occupational history, substance abuse history, and violence or abuse history;
   - living arrangements and circumstances, including location, quality, and stability of housing and household composition;
   - community-based supports, such as significant relationships (family and friends) and involvement in social, religious, and community organizations and activities;
   - physical and medical condition, including health status; health risks; and access to health care, nutrition, and medication;
   - behavior and behavioral challenges, including any evidence of violence;
   - emotional status, including mood and affect;
   - cognitive status, including an assessment of competence and any evidence of cognitive impairment, suicidal ideation, violent or homicidal ideation, or psychosis;
   - educational issues, including evidence of intellectual functioning, learning needs, and disabilities;
   - occupational issues, including employment challenges, special needs, and any disabilities;
   - financial issues, including both acute and chronic challenges;
   - legal issues, including domestic, civil, and criminal issues;
   - a global assessment of the person's level of functioning.

3. In light of the information you have gathered about the individual's or family's needs, status and circumstances, capacities, strengths, and challenges, what resources are available that might assist them?

Various ways exist to identify local human service resources. Many state and county departments of human services, as well as local chapters of the United Way, maintain up-to-date directories of services and programs. Such directories may be available both in print and on the Internet. Many states and communities also participate in the "2-1-1" information and referral service, which offers people in need the option of making a toll-free call to a comprehensive, professionally staffed information and referral program. Local United Way and Red Cross chapters or departments of human services may sponsor the 2-1-1 service.

4. What steps must be taken to connect the individual or family with the available resources? Keep in mind factors such as location, eligibility criteria, funding possibilities, and ways to facilitate access.

Some regions and communities offer a richer collection of human services programs than others do. In general, major metropolitan areas tend to have more options than smaller, more remote communities.

- Most programs require individuals and families to meet eligibility criteria to receive services. These criteria may relate to the nature of the presenting problem or need, mental health, physical disability, developmental disability, health status, current medications, income, financial assets, employment status and history, educational status and history, insurance coverage, legal residence, history of victimization, social service history, substance abuse history, sexual orientation, religion, ethnicity, age, gender, family composition, immigration status, and citizenship.

- Some agencies and programs can provide services to people who have little or no ability to pay for services. Such agencies and programs usually have funding contracts or grants from other government agencies, private companies, or foundations. Some programs rely at least partially on clients' ability to pay for services out of pocket or with insurance benefits.

- Simply handing someone in need the names, addresses, and telephone numbers of potential service providers often will not be enough to facilitate access. A common problem with this approach is that the person in need may feel so overwhelmed by the challenges he or she is facing that the person may have difficulty following through with the referral. Another common problem is that service providers may face such overwhelming demand that they turn potential consumers away or place new applicants on lengthy waiting lists. Professionals and volunteers can increase the likelihood that people in need will receive services if they take several concrete steps, including contacting service providers personally to facilitate the referral, arranging specific appointments for people in need, and following up with people in need to see whether they have contacted service providers.

Useful Resources

Human services professionals, volunteers, and consumers may obtain additional helpful information from a variety of sources. For your convenience, the balance of this introduction lists some of the most prominent information sources.

The Alliance of Information and Referral Systems (AIRS) was incorporated in 1973 to enhance access to human services by providing information and referrals through publications, international training conferences, and an information and referral clearinghouse. AIRS offers a professional umbrella for information and referral providers in public and private organizations throughout the United States. AIRS promotes the professional development of information and referral specialists, who assess callers' needs, determine their options and best course of action, direct them to appropriate programs or services, provide culturally appropriate support, intervene in crisis situations, and advocate for the caller as needed. Contact AIRS at 703-218-AIRS (2477) and http://www.airs.org.

The United Way of America (UWA) is the national organization of approximately 1,400 community-based United Way chapters throughout the United States. Each year the United Way raises funds through a capital campaign (donations) and other gifts such as planned giving, gifts to specific initiatives, corporate sponsorships, and government grants. Each local United Way is independent, separately incorporated, and governed by local volunteers. Many United Way chapters provide information and referral services. Contact UWA at 703-836-7112 and http://www.unitedway.org.

The American Red Cross sponsors a variety of critical services in local communities throughout the United States. Disaster services are offered in response to fires, hurricanes, floods, earthquakes, tornadoes, hazardous material spills, transportation accidents, and explosions; biomedical services include blood services, tissue services for transplantation, and plasma services; services to military members and families include emergency services, counseling, financial assistance, and telecommunications; health and safety services include lifesaving training and health education; international services center on emergency relief to disaster victims and humanitarian aid; and community services range from home-delivered meals, food pantries, rides to medical appointments, homeless shelters, transitional housing, caregiver education, support groups, and nursing home and hospital volunteers to friendly visiting, latchkey programs, fuel assistance, and language banks. Contact the American Red Cross at 202-303-4498 and http://www.redcross.org.

Several federal agencies offer human services. The most prominent federal agencies and important human services providers within them include

- U.S. Department of Health and Human Services
  - o Administration for Children and Families (ACF)
  - o Administration on Aging (AoA)
  - o Centers for Disease Control and Prevention (CDC)
  - o Centers for Medicare and Medicaid Services (CMS)
  - o Food and Drug Administration (FDA)
  - o Health Resources and Services Administration (HRSA)
  - o Indian Health Service (IHS)
  - o National Institutes of Health (NIH)
  - o Substance Abuse and Mental Health Services Administration (SAMHSA)

- U.S. Department of Housing and Urban Development
  - o Office of Community Planning and Development
  - o Government National Mortgage Association (Ginnie Mae)
  - o Multifamily housing support programs
  - o Office of Fair Housing and Equal Opportunity
  - o Office of Federal Housing Enterprise Oversight
  - o Office of Health Homes and Lead Hazard Control
  - o Office of Housing
  - o Office of Public and Indian Housing
- U.S. Department of Education
  - o Bilingual Education and Minority Language Affairs
  - o Office for Civil Rights
  - o Office of Elementary and Secondary Education
  - o Office of Postsecondary Education
  - o Office of Special Education and Rehabilitative Services
  - o Office of Student Financial Assistance
  - o Office of Vocational and Adult Education
- U.S. Department of Justice
  - o Bureau of Alcohol, Tobacco, Firearms, and Explosives
  - o Office of Community Oriented Policing Services
  - o Drug Enforcement Administration
  - o Executive Office for Immigration Review
  - o Federal Bureau of Prisons
  - o Office of Justice Programs
    - Bureau of Justice Assistance
    - Bureau of Justice Statistics
    - National Institute of Justice
    - Office of Juvenile Justice and Delinquency Prevention
    - Office for Victims of Crime
- U.S. Department of Labor
  - o Employee Benefits Security Administration
  - o Employment and Training Administration
  - o Office of Disability Employment Policy
  - o Occupational Safety and Health Administration
  - o Veterans' Employment and Training Service
  - o Women's Bureau

- U.S. Department of Veterans Affairs
  - o Veterans Health Administration
    - Blind Rehabilitation Service
    - Center for Women Veterans
    - Readjustment Counseling Service (provides services related to bereavement and posttraumatic stress)
    - Homeless veterans' services
    - Services for HIV/AIDS, cancer, diabetes, elder care, and mental health care
  - o Veterans Benefits Administration
    - programs and services related to compensation and pension, education, vocational rehabilitation and employment, survivors' and dependents' benefits, burial services, and medical services
- U.S. Department of Defense
  - o U.S. Army programs and services, including Army OneSource; a 24-hour counseling hotline; the Center for Health Promotion and Preventive Medicine; the Center for Substance Abuse programs; child and youth services; the Community and Family Support Center emergency relief; programs for families, including Families Online and the Army Family Action Plan; the Medical Department; and programs addressing health care, housing, legal services, and retirement services;
  - o U.S. Navy programs and services, including Navy OneSource, benefits, emergency services, family assistance, and housing;
  - o U.S. Air Force programs and services, including casualty and loss, education, elder care, family separations, financial information, parenting, a spouse network, suicide prevention, and programs for teenagers and youths
- U.S. Department of Agriculture
  - o Food, Nutrition, and Consumer Services
    - Women, Infants, and Children
    - Food Stamp Program
    - School Meals
    - Summer Food Service Program
    - Child and Adult Care Food Program

- Food Assistance for Disaster Relief
- Food Distribution (Schools/Child Nutrition Commodity Program, Food Distribution Program on Indian Reservations, Nutrition Services Incentive Program, Commodity Supplemental Food Program, Emergency Food Assistance Program).

o Rural Development Housing Program.

Independent and quasi-official federal agencies and corporations also offer numerous programs and services. These include

- Commission on Civil Rights
- Corporation for National and Community Service
- Equal Employment Opportunity Commission
- National Council on Disability
- Social Security Administration
- Legal Services Corporation.

State governments typically have independent departments and divisions responsible for human services, child welfare, elderly affairs, education, health, mental health, intellectual disability, disabilities, rehabilitation services, housing, veterans affairs, transportation, labor, emergency management, corrections, law enforcement, and professional licensure.

Local agencies may be public or private. Cities and towns often have local public offices that address issues related to human services, poverty, child welfare, elderly affairs, education, health, mental health, intellectual disability, disabilities, rehabilitation services, housing, veterans affairs, transportation, labor, emergency management, corrections, and law enforcement. Many communities also are served by privately run community mental health centers, family service agencies, and community action programs that provide a broad, comprehensive array of human services. Many private agencies specialize in delivering services related to poverty, child welfare, elderly affairs, education, health, mental health, intellectual disability, disabilities, rehabilitation services, addictions, reproductive rights, housing, veterans affairs, transportation, employment, immigration, and crisis intervention.

How to Use the Guide

The remaining sections of this guide are organized on the basis of critically important areas of need. Each section includes a brief summary of important information related to

- services and benefits
- eligibility criteria
- contact information
- useful tips and sources of information.

Income Support Programs

Overview

INCOME SUPPORT PROGRAMS provide financial assistance to people who live in poverty or who struggle to pay for basic needs such as food, housing, clothing, and health care. Assistance ranges from short-term financial aid to long-term support. Income support programs typically provide emergency financial assistance (grants), loans, monthly stipends, or tax credits. In addition, low-income people may be eligible for tax benefits that help them make ends meet. Prominent programs and options include

- Temporary Assistance for Needy Families (TANF)
- General Public Assistance
- Social Security Disability Insurance (SSDI)
- Supplemental Security Income (SSI)
- Retirement
- Unemployment Insurance (UI)
- Workers' Compensation
- Temporary Disability Insurance (TDI)
- National Child Support Enforcement (CSE) Program
- Federal Earned Income Tax Credit (EITC)
- Federal Child Tax Credit (CTC)
- "Circuit breaker" programs for elderly and disabled residents.

Temporary Assistance for Needy Families (TANF)

SERVICES AND BENEFITS

The time-limited TANF program assists families who have children when the parents or other responsible relatives cannot provide for the family's basic needs. The federal government provides grants to states, territories, and tribes to run the TANF program, which has four goals. TANF strives to

1. provide assistance to needy families so that children may be cared for in their own homes or in the homes of relatives
2. reduce the dependence of needy parents on government benefits by promoting job preparation, work, and marriage
3. prevent out-of-wedlock pregnancies
4. encourage the formation and maintenance of two-parent families.

ELIGIBILITY CRITERIA

States, territories, and tribes have broad flexibility to carry out their programs. Each state designs the program, the type and amount of assistance payments, the range of services to be provided, and the rules for determining eligibility. States, territories, and tribes have established eligibility criteria for financial assistance, health care, and child care. Eligibility typically is based on amount of earned and unearned income. Participants must comply with strict program guidelines related to employment, acceptable work activities, job preparation, education, and time limits for cash assistance.

CONTACT INFORMATION

Contact the state, territorial, or tribal agency responsible for administering TANF (for example, the department of human and social services). General information on TANF is available at http://www.acf.hhs.gov/programs/ofa/tanf/about.html.

General Public Assistance

SERVICES AND BENEFITS

Many states provide short-term cash assistance and medical benefits to low-income people.

ELIGIBILITY CRITERIA

States and local governments typically provide some form of emergency or short-term assistance in the form of cash, prescription medication, utility payments, or health care to needy individuals and families. Eligibility criteria vary, but eligibility generally is based on applicants' income and available resources, such as savings and an automobile.

CONTACT INFORMATION

Contact the state, county, city, or other government agency responsible for human and social services.

Social Security Disability Insurance (SSDI)

SERVICES AND BENEFITS

SSDI provides benefits to people who are disabled and who are "insured" by workers' contributions to the Social Security Trust Fund through the Federal Insurance Contributions Act (FICA) tax paid on their earnings.

ELIGIBILITY CRITERIA

SSDI pays benefits to insured individuals and certain members of their families (spouses and children). To qualify, a person must have a medical condition that meets the Social Security Administration's definition of long-term disability and must have been employed in a job covered by social security. People qualify for benefits based on the length of time they worked and paid social security taxes. "Disability" under Social Security is based on a person's inability to work. A person is disabled under Social Security rules if the person cannot do work that he or she did before, if the person cannot adjust to other work because of a medical condition, and if the disability has lasted or is expected to last for at least one year or to result in death.

CONTACT INFORMATION

Contact the local office of the Social Security Administration. General information on SSDI is available at http://www.ssa.gov/disability/.

Supplemental Security Income (SSI)

SERVICES AND BENEFITS

The SSI program makes cash assistance payments to elderly, blind, and disabled people, including children under age 18, who have limited income and resources. The federal government funds SSI from general tax revenues, not from social security taxes.

ELIGIBILITY CRITERIA

Eligibility is based on applicants' income (wages, social security benefits, workers compensation, pensions, unemployment benefits, money from friends and relatives, and free food and shelter) and assets (bank accounts, cash, stocks, and bonds).

CONTACT INFORMATION

Contact the local office of the Social Security Administration. General information on SSI is available at http://www.ssa.gov/ssi/.

Retirement Insurance

SERVICES AND BENEFITS

The Social Security Administration provides monthly retirement benefits to people (or beneficiaries) who have reached the required age and paid U.S. social security taxes. The retirement program is the largest social insurance program run by the Social Security Administration. The program provides monthly benefits that are designed to replace income lost through retirement, disability, or death.

ELIGIBILITY CRITERIA

People who work and pay social security taxes earn social security credits. The amount an individual will receive in Social Security benefits is based on the number of credits earned and the amount of earnings averaged over the course of that person's working career. Family members (widows, widowers, spouses, and children) may also be eligible to receive benefits.

CONTACT INFORMATION

Contact the local office of the Social Security Administration. General information on social security benefits is available at http://www.ssa.gov/pgm/links_retirement.htm.

Unemployment Insurance (UI)

SERVICES AND BENEFITS

UI benefits provide temporary income for workers who are unemployed through no fault of their own. The funding for UI benefits comes from taxes paid by employers.

ELIGIBILITY CRITERIA

Applicants for UI benefits must have earned a minimum income during a specified base period (for example, the first four of the past five completed calendar quarters).

CONTACT INFORMATION

Contact the state or other government agency responsible for administering the UI program (for example, the state department of labor).

Workers' Compensation

SERVICES AND BENEFITS

Workers' compensation provides medical treatment, wage replacement and permanent disability compensation to employees who suffer job-related injuries or illnesses, and death benefits to dependents of workers who have died as a result of their employment. Benefits may include medical treatment, temporary disability benefits, permanent partial benefits, permanent total benefits, supplemental job displacement benefits, vocational rehabilitation, and death benefits.

ELIGIBILITY CRITERIA

Workers are eligible if they suffer a job-related injury or occupational disease.

Contact the state or other government agency responsible for administering the Workers' Compensation program (for example, the state department, office, division, or bureau of workers' compensation).

Temporary Disability Insurance (TDI)

SERVICES AND BENEFITS
Some states provide financial assistance to people who are unable to work because of illness or injury.

ELIGIBILITY CRITERIA
TDI benefits ordinarily require that applicants experience a non–work-related disability. Applicants for TDI must have earned a minimum income during a specified base period (for example, the first four of the past five completed calendar quarters).

CONTACT INFORMATION
Contact the state or other government agency responsible for administering the TDI program (for example, the state department of labor).

Child Support Enforcement (CSE)

SERVICES AND BENEFITS
The CSE Program is a federal, state, and local partnership designed to help families by promoting family self-sufficiency and child well-being. Child support agencies locate noncustodial parents, establish paternity when necessary, establish orders for support, and collect child support payments for families. All states and some American Indian nations run CSE programs, through either the human services department or the department of revenue, often with the help of prosecuting attorneys, district attorneys, other law enforcement agencies, and officials of family or domestic relations courts. Families seeking government child support services must apply directly through their state or local agency or through one of the nations running the program.

ELIGIBILITY CRITERIA

Custodial parents who are not receiving child support may be eligible for assistance. Noncustodial parents who are not paying required child support may be subject to a variety of enforcement mechanisms, such as interception of tax refunds, wages, workers' compensation benefits, lottery winnings, and unemployment benefits; seizure of financial assets; property liens; and criminal charges.

CONTACT INFORMATION

Contact the state or local agency responsible for the CSE program (usually the state human services or social service agency). General information on child support enforcement is available at http://www.acf.hhs.gov/programs/cse/.

Tax Assistance

Low- and moderate-income people may qualify for a variety of tax breaks, such as the federal Earned Income Tax Credit (EITC), the federal Child Tax Credit, or state-sponsored "circuit breaker" programs.

Federal Earned Income Tax Credit

BENEFITS

The EITC is a special tax benefit for people who earn low or moderate incomes. It lowers their taxes, supplements their wages, and makes work more attractive and affordable. Qualifying people who file federal tax returns get back some or all of the federal income tax withheld from their pay during the year. Even workers whose earnings are too small to have taxes withheld can benefit from the EITC. Families with children who claim the federal EITC also may be eligible for a tax credit on their state income tax.

ELIGIBILITY CRITERIA

The EITC amount is based on income and family size. The EITC generally does not affect eligibility for other programs, such as Medicaid, SSI, food stamps, or low-income housing.

CONTACT INFORMATION

Contact the state, county, or local tax assessor, revenue department, or treasurer's office. General information on the EITC is available at http://www.irs.gov/individuals/article/0,,id=96466,00.html.

Federal Child Tax Credit

BENEFITS

The Child Tax Credit is a federal tax credit for families with children under age 17. The credit lessens the impact of income taxes for families raising children. Qualifying people who file federal tax returns get back some or all of the federal income tax withheld from their pay during the year. In addition, some workers whose earnings are too low to have taxes withheld can get cash back from the credit.

ELIGIBILITY CRITERIA

A child must be under the age of 17. Eligible children include a son, daughter, adopted child, stepchild or eligible foster child, brother, sister, stepbrother, stepsister, or a descendant of any of these individuals or other eligible person who lived in the household all year as a member of the household.

CONTACT INFORMATION

Contact the state, county, or local tax assessor, revenue department, or treasurer's office. General information on the Child Tax Credit is available at http://www.irs.gov/newsroom/article/0,,id=106182,00.html.

Circuit Breaker Programs

BENEFITS

Many states sponsor "circuit breaker" programs that provide eligible elderly, disabled, and other qualified residents with property tax reductions or rent rebates.

Eligibility Criteria

Eligibility criteria vary among state programs. Typical criteria for circuit breaker programs include age (for example, age 65 and older), evidence of disability, and low or moderate income.

Contact Information

Contact the state, county, or local tax assessor, revenue department, or treasurer's office.

Useful Tips

Some people who need income supports are unfamiliar with available programs or have difficulty advocating on their own behalf. Many different organizations, professionals, and volunteers are available to help people in need locate appropriate income support programs, apply for benefits, and process appeals. Examples include welfare rights organizations, community advocacy groups, legal aid clinics, disability centers, senior centers, and attorneys.

Housing Assistance Programs

Overview

EVERYONE NEEDS HOUSING and shelter. The kind of housing and shelter a person requires will vary depending on the person's life circumstances. A woman who is being battered by her husband needs emergency shelter in a confidential location. A man with mental illness who struggles with heroin addiction needs a residential program for people with so-called co-occurring disorders (mental illness and substance abuse). A young married couple with a child may be eager to buy their first home but lack sufficient money for a down payment. An elderly man whose wife just died may want to stay in the home the couple lived in for nearly 50 years but finds it difficult to make ends meet. A single mother who dropped out of high school may need to find an affordable apartment where she and her two children can live while she completes a vocational training program.

The effort to provide homes and shelter to diverse populations means that housing assistance programs take many forms. The best known forms of housing assistance are designed to help people who are homeless, victims of domestic violence, coping with mental illness and substance abuse, having difficulty affording high rents and home purchase prices, elderly, or physically disabled. Some programs provide housing-related supportive services, such as furniture banks and help with the cost of utilities (see the section on energy assistance).

Some housing assistance programs provide physical shelter. Other programs provide financial assistance or subsidies that help people make their rent payment, down payment, or mortgage payment. Prominent programs and services include

- emergency shelters
- subsidized housing programs targeting specific populations
- continuing care, nursing, or retirement programs
- furniture banks.

Emergency Shelters

SERVICES AND BENEFITS
Many communities offer emergency shelter services for special-needs populations. Emergency shelters often specialize in services for people who are homeless, victims of domestic violence, runaways, or struggling with mental illness or substance abuse.

ELIGIBILITY CRITERIA
Eligibility criteria vary widely. Most emergency shelters impose strict eligibility or intake criteria based on evidence that applicants are homeless, victims of domestic violence, runaways, or struggling with mental illness or substance abuse.

CONTACT INFORMATION
Sponsors of emergency shelters vary. Most shelters are operated by private nonprofit organizations, such as family service agencies, community action programs, and religious organizations, or by state and local government human services agencies. Contact local information and referral organizations and agencies that specialize in emergency services, such as police departments, housing agencies, domestic violence resource centers, substance abuse treatment programs, the American Red Cross, and hospital emergency rooms.

Subsidized Housing for Low-Income and Moderate-Income People

Several housing subsidy and housing assistance programs are available to help low- and moderate-income people. The most prominent programs involve federal subsidies. Some states also offer housing subsidies. Major subsidy programs include public housing and Section 8 housing.

Public Housing

SERVICES

Public housing programs usually are sponsored by county or city government agencies. Public housing takes many forms, including high-rise or garden-style apartments for low-income people and elderly or disabled people, and single-family homes in scattered sites. The U.S. Department of Housing and Urban Development (HUD) administers federal aid to local housing agencies that manage the housing for low-income residents.

ELIGIBILITY CRITERIA

Access to public housing is restricted to low-income individuals and families. Eligibility is based on annual gross income; an applicant's status as elderly, disabled, or a member of a qualifying family; and U.S. citizenship or appropriate immigration status. Depending on income, applicants may qualify for assistance in one of two categories: lower income or very low income. To qualify for the lower income category, applicants may earn no more than 80 percent of the median income for the county or metropolitan area in which they choose to live. To qualify for the very low income category, applicants may earn no more than 50 percent of the median income for the county or metropolitan area in which they choose to live. Actual income limits vary from area to area, which means that applicants may be eligible in one location but not another.

CONTACT INFORMATION

Contact the local public housing agency. A list of contacts is available from HUD at http://www.hud.gov/offices/pih/pha/contacts/ and from the Public Housing Authority Directors Association at http://www. phada.org/ha_list.php.

Section 8: Housing Choice Certificates and Vouchers

SERVICES
Housing certificates and vouchers allow very low income families to lease or purchase privately owned housing. Typically, the housing allowance is based on a percentage of income. Section 8 program funds are earmarked for rental assistance, homeownership, and housing rehabilitation.

ELIGIBILITY CRITERIA
Eligibility for rental assistance is based on income limits for different size households. Assistance with homeownership typically is based on household income.

CONTACT INFORMATION
Contact the local public housing authority that administers the Section 8 program or the state or local housing finance agency. A list of public housing contacts is available from HUD at http://www.hud.gov/offices/pih/ programs/hcv/index.cfm. A list of housing finance agencies is available from the National Council of State Housing Agencies at http://www. ncsha.org/section.cfm/4/39.

Subsidized Housing for Elderly People

Various housing subsidy programs are available to assist elderly people. Prominent programs include rent subsidies and reverse mortgages.

Rent Subsidies (Section 8 and Section 202)

SERVICES AND BENEFITS
Two rent subsidy programs include funds earmarked to assist elderly people. Under Section 8, the Housing Choice Voucher program allows

elderly people who have very low incomes to lease or purchase privately owned housing. Typically the housing allowance is based on a percentage of income. Section 8 programs are earmarked for rental assistance, home-ownership, and housing rehabilitation.

Under Section 202, the Supportive Housing for the Elderly program provides housing for elderly people with very low incomes. Rental assistance funds are available to cover the difference between what the renter can pay and the actual cost of the housing. Funds also can be used to provide supportive services.

ELIGIBILITY CRITERIA
Eligibility is based on income limits for different size households.

CONTACT INFORMATION
General information on housing options for elderly people is available from HUD at http://www.hud.gov/groups/seniors.cfm. For state and local information, contact state and local departments of elderly affairs, housing agencies, and area offices on aging.

Reverse Mortgages

SERVICES AND BENEFITS
Reverse mortgages are a unique form of home loan that allow elderly homeowners to convert the equity in their homes into cash. The cash drawn from the equity can be taken all at once (as a lump sum), as a regular monthly cash advance, or on an as-needed basis from a "credit line" account. The reverse mortgage loan need not be repaid while the borrower lives in the home. The loan is repaid at the time of the borrower's death, on the sale of the home, or on the borrower's permanent relocation.

ELIGIBILITY CRITERIA
People who have reached a certain age (for example, age 62) and who own their homes generally are eligible for reverse mortgage loans.

Contact private mortgage lenders and state housing finance agencies to obtain general information on reverse mortgages. Information on reverse mortgages for elderly people also can be obtained from HUD at http://www.hud.gov/buying/rvrsmort.cfm.

Subsidized Housing for People with Disabilities

Services and Benefits
The federal government and some state and local agencies sponsor subsidized housing programs for people with disabilities. The most prominent federal program is Section 811: Supportive Housing for People with Disabilities. This program provides housing subsidies that help enable low-income people with disabilities to live as independently as possible.

Eligibility Criteria
To live in Section 811 housing, a household must be considered very low income (earning at or below 50 percent of the median income for the area), and at least one member of the household must be age 18 or older and have a disability. The disability may be a physical or developmental disability or a chronic mental illness.

Contact Information
General information about subsidized housing for people with disabilities is available from HUD at http://www.hud.gov/offices/hsg/mfh/progdesc/disab811.cfm.

Subsidized Rural Housing

Services and Benefits
Several rent subsidy programs use funds earmarked for people who live in rural settings. Prominent programs include

- the Section 502 Direct Loan Program, which provides loans to people of low or moderate income for the purchase, construction, or rehabilitation of single-family homes in rural areas

- the Section 504 Home Repair Loan and Grant Program, which provides loans to make repairs of homes owned by low-income residents in rural areas
- the Section 514 and 516 Farm Labor Housing Program, which subsidizes development of rental housing for domestic farm laborers
- the Section 515 Rural Rental Housing Program, which provides loans for development of rental or cooperative housing in rural areas for low- and moderate-income people
- the Section 521 Rental Assistance Program, which provides direct rental assistance to low-income tenants in eligible rural housing settings.

ELIGIBILITY CRITERIA

Eligibility for loans and rental assistance is based on various factors, including income limits based on household size, home equity, and assets.

CONTACT INFORMATION

General information about rural housing assistance is available from the Housing Assistance Council at http://www.ruralhome.org/ and from HUD at http://www.hud.gov/.

Continuing Care, Nursing Homes, and Retirement Settings

SERVICES AND BENEFITS

Most communities offer a range of continuing care and retirement settings for elderly people or people who need some form of assistance or supportive services. Options include continuing care retirement communities, assisted-living facilities, and nursing homes.

Continuing care retirement housing communities, also called life care communities, typically have large campuses that include several "levels" of housing. These communities include housing for people who are able to live independently, assisted-living facilities for people who require more support, and nursing homes for people who need skilled nursing care. As their needs change, residents move from one housing level to another.

Assisted-living facilities that are not part of a continuing care community also are available. Assisted-living facilities typically provide supportive services for residents who need some assistance but do not require skilled nursing care. Common services include meals, housekeeping, transportation, laundry, help with dressing and grooming, and some help with medications.

Nursing homes provide skilled nursing care and rehabilitation services to people with illnesses, injuries, or functional disabilities. Most nursing homes serve elderly residents, although some nursing homes also serve younger people with special needs, such as developmental disabilities, mental illness, and addictions. Some nursing facilities provide intermediate care for residents who need some assistance with activities of daily living but do not need skilled nursing care on a 24-hour basis.

Eligibility Criteria

Continuing care retirement communities may require membership. Most such communities require applicants to undergo a comprehensive medical examination to assess their physical and mental status. Some continuing care retirement communities require residents to have Medicare coverage (Parts A and B). Residents must be able to afford the entrance fee and monthly payments.

Assisted-living facilities have diverse eligibility criteria related to mental status, physical status, and ability to pay. Most assisted-living facility residents pay out of pocket. Medicare does not cover the cost of assisted-living facilities, and state Medicaid programs may cover only limited services, if any.

Nursing home admission typically is based on a needs assessment that evaluates applicants' ability to care for themselves. The assessment considers the applicant's ability to manage tasks related to personal care, mobility, eating, toileting, laundry, transportation, housekeeping, medication, and other similar tasks. The needs assessment also considers the applicant's family and community supports, medical needs, physician recommendations, and degree of required supervision.

CONTACT INFORMATION

General information about continuing care, nursing care, and retirement settings can be obtained from a large number of public- and private-sector sponsors and from HUD at http://www.hud.gov/utilities/intercept.cfm? or from http://www.alternativesforseniors.com/.

Furniture Banks

SERVICES AND BENEFITS

Furniture banks typically are sponsored by nonprofit community-based agencies. Furniture banks distribute essential furnishings, such as living room furniture, bedroom furniture, and appliances to help homeless individuals and families establish a stable residence and prevent people from sleeping on the floor.

ELIGIBILITY CRITERIA

Eligibility criteria typically include a referral from an emergency shelter, transitional housing program, or other social services agency.

CONTACT INFORMATION

Contact local emergency shelters, transitional housing programs, public welfare offices, the United Way, and the American Red Cross.

Useful Tips

HUD maintains a list of approved housing counseling agencies in states and local communities. These agencies can provide useful information to people about emergency housing, rental subsidies, and affordable housing options. Information about housing-related counseling is available from HUD at http://www.hud.gov/offices/hsg/sfh/hcc/hcc_home.cfm.

Many states and communities sponsor public housing agencies and housing finance agencies that provide information and referrals about many housing options for low- and moderate-income people. A list of public housing contacts is available from HUD at http://www.hud.gov/offices/pih/pha/contacts/, and a list of housing finance agencies can be obtained from the National Council of State Housing Agencies at http://www.ncsha.org/.

Contact hospital social services and social work departments as well as state and county health departments and developmental disabilities agencies to obtain useful information about assisted-living facilities and nursing homes. Departments of elderly affairs also can provide useful information about nursing homes and reverse mortgages. Domestic violence resource centers and substance abuse treatment programs and clearinghouses can provide valuable information about housing options for people with these special needs.

Several national organizations conduct research and address policy issues related to affordable housing and homelessness. For more information, contact

- the Homelessness Resource Center (http://homelessness.samhsa.gov/Default.aspx)
- the National Alliance to End Homelessness (http://www.endhomelessness.org/)
- the National Coalition for the Homeless (http://www.nationalhomeless.org/)
- the National Law Center on Homelessness and Poverty (http://www.nlchp.org/)
- the National Housing Conference (http://www.nhc.org/)
- the National Housing Institute (http://www.nhi.org/)
- the National Low Income Housing Coalition (http://www.nlihc.org/)
- the Council for Affordable and Rural Housing (http://www.carh.org/)
- the Joint Center for Housing Studies (http://www.jchs.harvard.edu/).

Food Assistance
Programs

Overview

FOOD IS ONE of life's most basic needs. Many people cannot afford food or have difficulty maintaining a nutritious diet. People who are homeless may depend on soup kitchens or scrounge in dumpsters for food. Low-income parents may serve their children food that is filling (high in carbohydrates) but not particularly nutritious. Elderly people on fixed incomes may skip meals to save money, people with physical disabilities may miss meals because they have difficulty traveling to a supermarket, and low-income children who have access to subsidized lunches during the school year may suffer nutritionally during the summer months. Fortunately, a variety of food subsidy and nutrition programs are available to people in need.

Food Banks and Food Rescue Organizations

SERVICES AND BENEFITS
Food banks and food rescue organizations typically accept donations of food from local grocery stores, farms, government agencies, food manufacturers and retailers, and private individuals. Food banks process, organize, and distribute food to soup kitchens and food rescue organizations in local communities. Food rescue organizations, such as food pantries, make food available to people in need.

ELIGIBILITY CRITERIA

People in need are referred to food rescue organizations from diverse sources, including emergency shelters, domestic violence programs, hospitals, religious organizations, and schools. Most food rescue organizations impose no eligibility criteria or have minimal eligibility criteria.

CONTACT INFORMATION

Contact information and referral agencies such as the United Way, the American Red Cross, hospital social work and social service departments, religious organizations, police departments, and local departments of human services to obtain information about locally available food rescue organizations. The national organization Feeding America sponsors an online resource to locate food banks throughout the United States (http://feedingamerica.org/foodbank-results.aspx).

Soup Kitchens

SERVICES AND BENEFITS

Soup kitchens typically are sponsored by nonprofit, community-based human services agencies or religious organizations and provide free meals to people in need.

ELIGIBILITY CRITERIA

Soup kitchens generally do not screen participants or assess their eligibility.

CONTACT INFORMATION

Contact information and referral agencies such as the United Way, the American Red Cross, hospital social work and social service departments, religious organizations, police departments, and local departments of human services to obtain information about local soup kitchens. The national organization Feeding America sponsors an online resource to locate soup kitchens and meal sites throughout the United States: http://feedingamerica.org/foodbank-results.aspx.

Food Subsidy Programs

SERVICES AND BENEFITS
The national Supplemental Nutrition Assistance Program (SNAP) helps individuals and families buy food and provide nutritional meals for themselves. The program may not be used to purchase tobacco, alcoholic beverages, pet food, paper or soap products, vitamins and medicines, hot foods, or foods that will be eaten in the store. Although the federal government oversees SNAP nationally through the U.S. Department of Agriculture (USDA), state and local welfare offices operate the program.

ELIGIBILITY CRITERIA
Eligibility for SNAP is based on individual or family income; available resources, such as money, investments, or ownership of an automobile; and family size.

CONTACT INFORMATION
Contact information for the state or local human services or welfare agency that administers SNAP is available at http://www.fns.usda.gov/fsp/contact_info/hotlines.htm. General information about SNAP is available at http://www.fns.usda.gov/fsp/.

Emergency Food Assistance Program

SERVICES AND BENEFITS
The Emergency Food Assistance Program distributes surplus commodities to low-income households and local emergency feeding organizations. Available foods—such as vegetables, fruits, meats, juice, dry beans, grains, cereals, and eggs—vary depending on market conditions.

ELIGIBILITY CRITERIA
Each state determines criteria for household eligibility and may adjust income criteria based on need in the state. Eligibility criteria may include participation in existing food or other assistance programs for which income is considered as a basis for eligibility.

CONTACT INFORMATION

Contact information for the emergency food providers that distribute surplus commodities is available at an online resource sponsored by Feeding America (http://feedingamerica.org/foodbank-results.aspx).

Meals on Wheels

SERVICES AND BENEFITS

Community-based Meals on Wheels programs deliver nutritious meals to people who are unable to leave their home to shop for groceries or who are unable to prepare their own meals. Some Meals on Wheels programs sponsor congregate meal sites.

ELIGIBILITY CRITERIA

Meals on Wheels programs typically serve people who are at least age 60 or who are coping with a serious injury, illness, or disability. Some programs consider participants' income and encourage meal recipients to make a modest monetary contribution toward the cost of meals and program administration.

CONTACT INFORMATION

Contact local social service and human service organizations that serve the elderly population and people with disabilities to obtain information about local Meals on Wheels programs. Such organizations may include area offices on aging, rehabilitation programs, hospital social service and social work departments, visiting nurses programs, home health care agencies, and local chapters of the American Red Cross. Local Meals on Wheels programs are independent programs. The Meals on Wheels Association of America sponsors an online resource to locate Meals on Wheels programs throughout the United States (http://www.mowaa.org/Page. aspx?pid=253).

Special Supplemental Nutrition Program for Women, Infants, and Children

SERVICES AND BENEFITS

The USDA's Special Supplemental Nutrition Program for Women, Infants, and Children (WIC) provides nutritious food to low-income women, infants, and children. The target populations include pregnant women, breastfeeding women, non-breastfeeding postpartum women, infants, and children up to age five. The program provides supplemental nutritious foods, nutrition education and counseling, and screening and referrals to other health and social services.

ELIGIBILITY CRITERIA

Eligibility is based on income guidelines, state residency requirements, and criteria for being considered at "nutritional risk."

CONTACT INFORMATION

Contact the state or local agency that is responsible for administering the WIC program. The USDA sponsors an online resource to locate WIC services throughout the United States (http://www.fns.usda.gov/wic/Contacts/statealpha.HTM).

National School Breakfast Program

SERVICES AND BENEFITS

The USDA's School Breakfast Program is a federally assisted meal program that provides cash assistance to states to operate nonprofit breakfast programs in schools and child care institutions. The program provides low-cost or free nutritional breakfasts to children each school day.

ELIGIBILITY CRITERIA

Eligibility for free or reduced-price meals is based primarily on family income in relation to the federal poverty level.

CONTACT INFORMATION
Contact local school district offices. Not all school districts participate in the program.

National School Lunch Program

SERVICES AND BENEFITS
The USDA's National School Lunch Program is a federally assisted meal program operating in public and nonprofit private schools and residential child care institutions. The program provides low-cost or free nutritious lunches to children each school day.

ELIGIBILITY CRITERIA
Eligibility for free or reduced-price meals is based primarily on family income in relation to the federal poverty level.

CONTACT INFORMATION
Contact local school district offices. Not all school districts participate in the program.

Special Milk Program for Children

SERVICES AND BENEFITS
The USDA's Special Milk Program provides milk to children in schools and child care institutions who do not participate in other federal meal service programs. The program reimburses schools for the milk they serve. Schools in the National School Lunch or School Breakfast Programs may also participate in the Special Milk Program to provide milk to children in half-day prekindergarten and kindergarten programs where children do not have access to the school meal programs.

ELIGIBILITY CRITERIA
Eligibility for free or reduced-price meals is based primarily on family income in relation to the federal poverty level.

CONTACT INFORMATION
Contact local school district offices. Not all school districts participate in the program.

Child and Adult Care Food Program

SERVICES AND BENEFITS

The USDA's Child and Adult Care Food Program (CACFP) provides food to low-income families, including adults who receive care in nonresidential adult day care centers and children residing in homeless shelters. The program also provides snacks and supper to youths participating in eligible after-school programs.

ELIGIBILITY CRITERIA

Eligibility criteria vary according to the participant's status and program site. For example, children who live in homeless shelters or who participate in the Temporary Assistance for Needy Families program, Head Start, or the USDA's Food Distribution Program on Indian Reservations may be automatically eligible. Adults who participate in SNAP, SSI, or Medicaid programs may be automatically eligible. Participants also may need to meet income guidelines.

CONTACT INFORMATION

Contact the state or local human services or health agency that is authorized to administer the CACFP.

Summer Food Service Program

SERVICES AND BENEFITS

The USDA's Summer Food Service Program (SFSP) ensures that children in lower income communities continue to receive nutritious meals during long school vacations, when they do not have access to school breakfast or lunch.

ELIGIBILITY CRITERIA

All children 18 years and younger who come to an approved site may receive meals. Sites must be located in low-income communities or must serve primarily low-income children. At camps, only the children who are eligible for free or reduced-price meals may receive SFSP meals.

CONTACT INFORMATION

Contact state and local agencies that sponsor and administer the SFSP. Such agencies may include local schools, community centers, recreation centers and faith-based organizations. Not all communities participate in the program.

Useful Tips

Valuable information about federally funded food programs is available from the USDA's Food and Nutrition Service (http://www.fns.usda.gov/fns/). Prominent private organizations that address issues of hunger include

- Feeding America, a national organization that distributes food and grocery products through a nationwide network of certified affiliates, increases public awareness about hunger, and advocates for policies that address hunger (http://feedingamerica.org/)
- Food Research and Action Center, a national organization that promotes policies that address hunger and malnutrition in America (http://www.frac.org/)
- Share Our Strength, a national organization that mobilizes thousands of people in the culinary industry to organize antihunger events, host dinners, teach cooking classes to low-income individuals and families, and promote policies that address hunger and poverty (http://www.strength.org/).

CLOTHING ASSISTANCE PROGRAMS

Overview

MANY LOW-INCOME PEOPLE cannot afford adequate clothing, including typical day-to-day attire, underwear, and warm coats and jackets. Various programs are available in local communities to provide clothing assistance.

Clothing Allowances and Vouchers

SERVICES AND BENEFITS
Many state economic security programs provide publicly financed clothing allowances or vouchers for low-income families. Typical benefits include an annual clothing allowance or vouchers for children and adults who are making the transition from public assistance to employment.

ELIGIBILITY CRITERIA
Eligibility typically is based on the criteria for participation in economic security programs such as TANF and SSI.

CONTACT INFORMATION
Contact the state or local agencies authorized to administer economic security and public assistance programs. Such agencies may include state human service agencies and local public welfare departments.

Clothing Closets and Exchanges

Services and Benefits

Many nonprofit social service and religious organizations sponsor clothing closets and exchanges for people in need. Clothing closets operate all year, accepting donations of usable clothing and displaying them to the public in a store-like fashion. Clothing exchanges often are scheduled to occur twice each year. At a clothing exchange, participants are invited to donate usable clothing and select clothing from available stock; donations are not required.

Eligibility Criteria

Clothing exchanges and clothing closets typically do not screen consumers.

Contact Information

Contact local Salvation Army Thrift Stores, Goodwill stores, and storefronts sponsored by local nonprofit and religious organizations. Local organizations also may sponsor seasonal clothing exchanges.

Useful Tips

Information about nationally sponsored clothing assistance programs is available from

- Goodwill Industries International, Inc. (http://www.goodwill.org/)
- The Salvation Army (http://www.salvationarmyusa.org).

Information about clothing allowances and vouchers that are permitted under federally authorized economic security programs is available from the U.S. Department of Health and Human Services (http://www.acf.hhs.gov/) and from state and local human services agencies that sponsor economic security and public assistance programs.

Several national organizations monitor and advocate for clothing allowances and vouchers authorized under federal and state economic security programs. For more information, contact

- the Center for Law and Social Policy (http://www.clasp.org/)
- the Center on Budget and Policy Priorities (http://www.cbpp.org/)
- the Children's Defense Fund (http://www.childrensdefense.org/)
- the Institute for Research on Poverty (http://www.irp.wisc.edu/)
- the Program on Poverty and Social Welfare Policy (http://www.fordschool.umich.edu/research/poverty/).

Energy Assistance Programs

Overview

PEOPLE IN NEED sometimes struggle to afford basic utilities, such as heat and electricity. People who cannot afford to heat their homes suffer during cold weather. People who cannot afford electricity are unable to cook or refrigerate food, stay cool during intense heat waves, operate electric medical or other personal appliances, or turn on electric lights. Two major energy assistance programs are available to help people in need: the U.S. Department of Health and Human Services' (HHS) Low Income Home Energy Assistance Program (LIHEAP) and the U.S. Department of Energy's (DOE) Weatherization Assistance Program.

Low-Income Home Energy Assistance Program

SERVICES AND BENEFITS

LIHEAP is a federally funded program designed to help low-income households meet their home heating and cooling needs. The principal aim of the program is to provide energy assistance to reduce the risk of health and safety problems, such as illness, fire, or eviction. LIHEAP can provide financial assistance toward a household's energy bill, emergency assistance if a household's home energy service is shut off or about to be shut off, and a range of other energy-related services that states may choose to offer, such as weatherization improvements, utility equipment repair and replacement, budgeting counseling, and so forth.

The federal government does not provide energy assistance directly to the public. Rather, the federal government supports programs operated by state agencies, American Indian nations, and territorial agencies.

ELIGIBILITY CRITERIA

Eligibility typically is based on household income. LIHEAP grantees have the flexibility of serving only those income-eligible households that meet additional LIHEAP eligibility criteria, such as passing an assets test, living in nonsubsidized housing; having a household member who is elderly, disabled, or young; or receipt of a utility disconnection notice.

CONTACT INFORMATION

Contact the state or local agency authorized to administer the LIHEAP program. Examples include state energy assistance agencies or local community action programs.

Weatherization Assistance

SERVICES AND BENEFITS

Sponsored by the DOE, the Weatherization Assistance Program provides weatherization services to low-income households. The program helps people make energy-efficient improvements, such as installing storm windows, adding insulation, sealing cracks, installing weather stripping, repairing windows and doors, and repairing or enhancing heating systems. The program assists individuals, including elderly people and people with disabilities, and families through a network of partnerships with local weatherization agencies. Some states also fund energy assistance programs.

ELIGIBILITY CRITERIA

Eligibility is based primarily on household income. Age, disability, and participation in economic security programs such as SSI and TANF also may be considered.

DOE regional offices award grants to state agencies, which then contract with local agencies to operate energy assistance programs. Contact state and local energy assistance agencies, such as state energy offices and community action programs, for additional information about local programs.

Useful Tips

HHS sponsors an online and toll-free telephone service to help people locate LIHEAP programs. Information is available at http://www.acf.hhs.gov/programs/ocs/liheap/consumer_info/index.html. The LIHEAP Web site offers information on low-income energy issues related to

- state, American Indian nation, and territorial LIHEAP grantees
- community action agency and local government office subgrantees
- low-income energy service organizations
- fuel funds
- utilities and utility regulatory commissions.

The Weatherization Assistance Program Technical Assistance Center provides important information about energy assistance, weatherization, regulations, services, and contacts. Additional information is available at http://www.waptac.org/. The National Community Action Foundation sponsors an online service to help people locate the names and locations of local community action programs (http://www.ncaf.org/).

TRANSPORTATION
ASSISTANCE PROGRAMS

Overview

PEOPLE IN NEED often have difficulty arranging for basic transportation. Low-income people may not be able to afford an automobile or taxicab fare and may live a long distance from public transportation. Elderly people and people with disabilities may have difficulty with the physical challenges involved in driving or getting to a bus stop. Children and adults may have to travel long distances for emergency and time-critical medical care.

Elderly Transportation

SERVICES AND BENEFITS
Many communities offer transportation services to assist elderly people in getting to and from medical appointments, such as doctor's visits, kidney dialysis, and medical tests; senior day care; senior lunches; religious services and events; and grocery shopping. The local public transportation authority or volunteer groups, such as religious organizations or associations of retired people, may offer free or reduced-fare transportation services.

ELIGIBILITY CRITERIA
Eligibility for free and reduced-fare transportation services may be based on age, disability, and income. People who qualify for Medicaid may be eligible. Federal funds are apportioned to states under the Section 5310

(Title 49 U.S.C.) program administered by the Federal Transit Administration (FTA).

CONTACT INFORMATION
Contact state and local public transportation authorities, departments of elderly affairs, and area offices on aging for more information about transportation assistance available to elderly people.

Transportation for People with Disabilities

SERVICES AND BENEFITS
Many communities offer transportation services to assist people with disabilities in getting to and from medical appointments, such as doctor's visits, medical tests, and rehabilitation; day treatment programs; religious services and events; and grocery shopping. The local public transportation authority or volunteer groups, such as religious organizations or associations of retired people, may offer free or reduced-fare transportation services.

ELIGIBILITY CRITERIA
Many people with disabilities are eligible for "paratransit" (curb-to-curb) services under the Americans with Disabilities Act. Eligibility for transportation services may be based on disability and income. People who qualify for Medicaid may be eligible. Federal funds are apportioned to states under the Section 5310 (Title 49 U.S.C.) program administered by the FTA.

CONTACT INFORMATION
Contact state and local public transportation authorities and agencies that serve people with disabilities for more information about transportation assistance available to people with disabilities.

Air Transportation for Health Care

SERVICES AND BENEFITS
Several organizations offer free or reduced-cost air transportation to people who need critically important health care far from home. Using a

network of volunteer pilots, these organizations provide transportation in pilots' personal general aviation aircraft. Transportation services also may be available on corporate jets. Pilots may transport organs, blood, tissue, or medical supplies, or transport patients who have urgent or time-critical needs, such as organ transplant patients.

ELIGIBILITY CRITERIA

Typical eligibility criteria include financial need, medical need, whether the individual is ambulatory and in stable medical condition, medical release from a physician, advance notice, and geographic location.

CONTACT INFORMATION

Several prominent organizations offer free or reduced-fare transportation for health care purposes. Contact

- Air Charity Network (http://aircharitynetwork.org/)
- Angel Flight (http://www.angelflight.org/)
- Children's Flight of Hope (http://www.childrensflightofhope.org/)
- Corporate Angel Network (http://www.corpangelnetwork.org/)
- LifeLine Pilots (http://www.lifelinepilots.org)
- Mercy Medical Airlift (http://www.mercymedical.org/)
- Faith Charity Flights USA (http://www.faithcharityflightsusa.org/).

Useful Tips

Information about free or reduced-fare transportation for people who are elderly or disabled is available from local public transportation authorities and public and private agencies that serve these populations. Information about time-critical transportation for health care needs is available from the National Patient Travel Center (http://www.patienttravel.org/). This organization provides information about all charitable long-distance medical air transportation and provides referrals within the national charitable medical air transportation network. Hospital social work departments may also provide useful information.

HEALTH CARE SERVICES

Overview

HEALTH CARE SERVICES rank among the most important services in people's lives. People in need often have great difficulty locating and paying for quality care.

Health care services correspond to a diverse set of needs that range from sudden, acute illnesses and medical emergencies to long-term, chronic conditions such as blindness, developmental disabilities, dementia, or terminal illnesses. Health care needs arise during every stage of life from birth through old age.

Maternal and Child Health

SERVICES AND BENEFITS

Maternal and child health services typically strive to

- reduce infant mortality and the incidence of disabling conditions among children, such as those that result from lead poisoning, asthma, or parental neglect or abuse
- increase the number of children immunized against disease
- increase the number of children who receive assessments and follow-up diagnostic and treatment services
- provide and ensure access to comprehensive perinatal care for women; preventive and child care services; comprehensive care, including long-term care services, for children with special health

care needs; and rehabilitation services for blind and disabled children
- facilitate the development of comprehensive, family-centered, community-based, culturally competent, coordinated systems of care for children with special health care needs.

Eligibility Criteria
Federal and state funds contribute to maternal and child health programs, such as the Title V (Social Security Act) Maternal and Child Health Services Block Grant, Medicaid, the Children's Health Insurance Program, the Healthy Start Program, the Emergency Medical Services for Children Program, and the WIC Program. States also play an important role in administering these programs. Eligibility criteria vary according to the funded programs and funding sources.

Contact Information
Contact state and local health departments, federal health care and human services agencies, hospitals, and other public and private agencies that administer maternal and child health programs for comprehensive information about maternal and child health.

Reproductive Health Care

Services and Benefits
Many health care agencies and organizations provide services related to reproduction. Services typically address

- adolescent sexuality
- assisted reproduction technology (ART)
- behavioral risk factors, such as smoking, nutrition, and substance abuse
- cervical cancer
- family planning
- gender-based violence
- HIV/AIDS
- hysterectomy

- infertility
- men's reproductive health
- pregnancy, pregnancy prevention, and pregnancy termination
- reproductive tract infections
- sexual and reproductive rights
- sexual education
- sexually transmitted infections
- tubal sterilization and vasectomy.

ELIGIBILITY CRITERIA
Eligibility criteria vary according to programs and funding resources.

CONTACT INFORMATION
Contact state and local health departments, health care clinics, family planning clinics, women's health care programs, physicians, and hospitals. Information about reproductive health and health care services is available from a wide range of public and private agencies.

Nutrition

SERVICES AND BENEFITS
Various federal, state, and local programs are available to enhance nutrition among infants, children, adolescents, adults, and elderly people. Examples of specific programs include nutrition education, breastfeeding, and cultural and ethnic resources. Programs receive funding from a combination of federal, state, and local sources.

ELIGIBILITY CRITERIA
Eligibility criteria vary according to programs and funding resources.

CONTACT INFORMATION
Contact nutrition programs sponsored by state and local health departments, federal health care and human services agencies, health care clinics, hospitals, schools, senior centers, community action programs, public welfare agencies, and other social service agencies.

Developmental Disabilities

SERVICES AND BENEFITS
Health care services and related social services are available to assist people with a wide range of developmental disabilities, such as

- Asperger's syndrome
- attention deficit disorder
- autism
- brain injury and malformation
- cerebral palsy
- communication, speech, and language disorders
- developmental delays
- Down's syndrome
- eating disorders
- feeding disorders
- fetal alcohol syndrome
- fragile X syndrome
- genetic disorders
- hearing impairment
- lead poisoning
- learning disorders
- mental retardation
- metabolic disorders
- neurological disorders
- seizure disorders
- skeletal disorders
- sleep disorders
- spina bifida
- spinal injuries.

ELIGIBILITY CRITERIA
Eligibility criteria vary depending on the nature of the disorder being treated, the treatment provider, available health insurance coverage, and funding sources.

Contact local hospitals, federal health care and human services agencies, health care clinics, and institutes that specialize in the treatment of developmental disorders. Information also is available from the developmental disabilities council in each state and territory. Developmental disabilities councils are charged with developing statewide plans to address the needs of people with developmental disabilities.

Physical Disabilities

SERVICES AND BENEFITS
Inpatient and outpatient health care and rehabilitation services, and related social services, are available to assist people with a wide range of physical disabilities, such as

- amputation
- brain trauma, tumors, and malformations
- burns
- cardiac diseases
- chronic pain
- musculoskeletal disorders
- neurological disorders, such as multiple sclerosis, muscular dystrophy, Parkinson's disease, and polyneuropathy
- orthopedic disorders and injuries
- polio
- respiratory diseases
- rheumatic diseases
- sexual disorders
- stroke
- urological disorders.

ELIGIBILITY CRITERIA
Eligibility criteria vary depending on the nature of the disability being treated, the treatment provider, available health insurance coverage, and funding sources.

Contact state, federal, and local health care and human services agencies; local hospitals; health care clinics; and institutes that specialize in the treatment of physical disabilities. Information also is available from the developmental disabilities council in each state and territory. Developmental disabilities councils are charged with developing statewide plans to address the needs of people with developmental disabilities.

Adult Day Care

SERVICES AND BENEFITS
Adult day care centers provide supportive services for people with cognitive and functional disabilities. Typical services include occupational therapy; physical therapy; speech therapy; counseling and case management services; health and medication monitoring; social activities; exercise; assistance with eating, walking, and toileting; and personal care.

ELIGIBILITY CRITERIA
Eligibility criteria vary depending on the nature of the services provided, consumers' needs, the treatment provider, available health insurance coverage, and funding sources.

CONTACT INFORMATION
Contact local area offices on aging, departments of elderly affairs, and senior centers for information about adult day care services. The National Association of Professional Geriatric Care Managers helps people locate a professional care manager (http://www.caremanager.org/).

Home Health Care and Respite Services

SERVICES AND BENEFITS
Home health care agencies provide supportive services in the home. Typical services include nursing, occupational therapy, physical therapy, social work, caregiver counseling, patient education, phlebotomy, wound care, medication training and compliance, and management of intravenous

treatments. Some programs also provide homemaker services for people who are ill or disabled. Typical homemaker services include preparing meals, house cleaning, running errands, facilitating appointments, and providing companionship.

Many home health care agencies also offer respite services. Respite care provides short-term assistance in blocks of time that offer family members and caregivers breaks from the stress of caring for a family member.

ELIGIBILITY CRITERIA

Eligibility criteria vary depending on the nature of the services provided, consumers' needs, the treatment provider, available health insurance coverage, and funding sources. Medicare, many private health insurance programs, and state-sponsored Medicaid programs cover home health services.

CONTACT INFORMATION

Contact local home health care agencies, such as visiting nurses, hospitals, area offices on aging, community health clinics, and senior centers for information about home health care services and respite care. Diverse agencies and programs, including traditional home health care agencies, religious organizations, and chapters of national organizations such as United Cerebral Palsy, the Easter Seal Society, and The Arc sponsor respite care. The National Association of Professional Geriatric Care Managers helps people locate a professional care manager (http://www.caremanager.org/).

Assisted Living

SERVICES AND BENEFITS

Assisted-living facilities provide a combination of housing, supportive services, and health care services to residents who need assistance with activities of daily living. In addition to housing, typical services include

- access to health and medical services
- assistance with eating, bathing, dressing, toileting, and walking

- emergency call systems for each resident's unit
- health promotion and exercise programs
- housekeeping services
- meals served in a common dining area
- medication management
- personal laundry services
- social and recreational activities
- transportation
- 24-hour security and staff availability.

Eligibility Criteria

Eligibility criteria vary depending on the facility. Some assisted-living facilities require significant entry fees and monthly payments. Most residents pay for services from their own financial resources. Limited coverage may be available for low-income people who are elderly and for people who are eligible for SSI and Medicaid.

Contact Information

Contact the local area office on aging and hospital-based social work departments for information about locally available assisted-living facilities. The National Association of Professional Geriatric Care Managers helps people locate a professional care manager (http://www.caremanager.org/).

Services for People with Alzheimer's Disease

Services and Benefits

Health care services and related social services are available to assist people with Alzheimer's disease. Services are designed to help with daily care (for example, communication, eating, incontinence, depression, dressing and grooming, dental and health care, late-stage care); managing behavior (for example, aggression, agitation, confusion, sleeplessness and sundowning, wandering); safety (for example, home safety, medication safety, driving, wandering); coping (for example, strategies for caregiver stress, changing relationships, grief and loss, getting respite); and caregiver stress.

Eligibility criteria vary depending on the nature of the services provided, consumers' needs, the treatment provider, available health insurance coverage, and funding sources. Medicare, many private health insurance programs, and state-sponsored Medicaid programs cover home health services.

CONTACT INFORMATION

Contact local health care agencies, such as visiting nurses, hospitals, area offices on aging, community health clinics, religious organizations, and senior centers for information about services for people with Alzheimer's disease. The Alzheimer's Association provides electronic links to information about conducting a needs assessment, exploring care options, coordinating care, finding local chapters, and locating supports (http://www.alz.org/carefinder/index.asp). The Eldercare Locator, sponsored by the U.S. Department of Health and Human Services (HHS), provides useful information about local agencies, in every U.S. community, that can help older people and their families access home and community-based services, such as transportation, meals, home care, and caregiver support services (http://www.eldercare.gov/Eldercare.NET/Public/Home.aspx). The National Association of Professional Geriatric Care Managers helps people locate a professional care manager (http://www.caremanager.org/). The National Academy of Elder Law Attorneys helps people locate lawyers who specialize in legal issues that sometimes arise when caring for someone with Alzheimer's disease (for example, advance directives, wills, estate planning) (http://www.naela.org/).

Nursing Homes

SERVICES AND BENEFITS

Nursing homes provide a range of health care and social services to help residents cope with illness or disabilities. Typical services include skilled nursing care and rehabilitation services, such as physical, occupational, speech, and respiratory therapy, for people with illnesses, injuries, or functional disabilities. Specialty care often is available related to treatment for

- Alzheimer's disease
- cancer
- cardiovascular disease
- developmental disability
- dementia
- head trauma
- hematologic conditions
- mental disease
- neurological disease
- neuromuscular diseases
- orthopedic rehabilitation
- pain therapy
- pulmonary disease
- paraplegic or quadriplegic impairments
- stroke recovery
- trauma
- wound care.

ELIGIBILITY CRITERIA

Most nursing homes serve elderly residents. Some nursing homes provide services to younger people with special needs, such as developmental disabilities, mental illness, and substance abuse. Many residents pay for nursing home services from their own financial resources. Some residents qualify for Medicare or Medicaid coverage.

CONTACT INFORMATION

Contact state and local health departments, hospital social service departments, area offices on aging, developmental disabilities councils, and senior centers for information about nursing homes.

Services for People with Visual Impairments

SERVICES AND BENEFITS

Various services are available to assist people who are blind or visually impaired. Typical services include

- assistive technology services using computer screen readers; magnification devices; Braille translation software or embossers; scanning devices; notetakers; or any item or piece of equipment that increases, maintains, or improves the functional ability of people with visual impairments
- independent home management skills training that focuses on practical skills, such as pouring liquids; writing checks; housekeeping; home repairs; food preparation; telling time; reading and writing; home safety; putting on make-up; and organizing and labeling medications, clothing, and toiletries
- low-vision services that help with magnification and lighting for people whose vision loss cannot be corrected with conventional glasses, contact lenses, surgery, or medication
- orientation and mobility training that helps people learn how to travel safely and independently, and which may include sensory training, use of a white cane, self-protection techniques, use of a sighted guide or dog guide, and instruction in the use of public transportation
- social work services, such as mental health counseling for people who are having difficulty adjusting to their blindness and assistance with quality-of-life issues related to housing, education, employment, child care, financial aid and public assistance, health care, and so on
- services for school-age children to coordinate the efforts of schools, state and local government agencies, families, and other community agencies that assess and treat vision-related disabilities
- specialized services to assist elderly people who suffer from vision-related disability resulting from diseases such as macular degeneration, diabetic retinopathy, cataracts, and glaucoma
- vocational services, such as training on assistive technology, vocational counseling, educational counseling, job-retention assistance, low-vision evaluations, and computer training to help blind people seek and maintain employment.

ELIGIBILITY CRITERIA

Eligibility criteria vary depending on the nature of the services provided, consumers' needs, the treatment provider, available health insurance coverage, and funding sources.

CONTACT INFORMATION

Contact public and private agencies at the state and local levels that provide assistance to people who are blind or visually impaired. Examples of such agencies include state and county agencies for the blind and visually impaired, and diverse nonprofit agencies. The American Federation for the Blind helps people locate services related to advocacy, assessment, assistive technology, braille, audio or large-print production, business services, community outreach programs, computer training, counseling, distance education, dog guide training, early intervention (infants), education services, employment and job training, financial assistance, health and fitness, health services, housing services, in-home services, information and referral, legal services, library services, low-vision services, orientation and mobility, parent assistance, preschool programs, reading services, recreation services, rehabilitation services, services for seniors, support services, transportation services, volunteer services (http://www.afb.org/services.asp).

Services for People with Hearing Impairments

SERVICES AND BENEFITS

Various services are available to assist people who are deaf or hearing impaired. Typical services include

- assistive technology, such as teletypwriters (TTYs), telecommunications devices for the deaf (TDDs), the telecommunications relay service, hearing aids, and other assistive listening device
- independent living services, involving training in practical skills that enable people with hearing impairments to live in their own homes
- interpreter services, including information about available services and referrals
- educational services to help people who are deaf or hearing impaired enroll in and complete educational programs, or to help facilitate reasonable accommodations
- mental health services that include individual, family, couples, and group counseling to help people cope with deafness and hearing impairment
- sign language instruction, including information about available services and referrals

- substance abuse services that include counseling and treatment related to drug abuse, alcohol abuse, and pathological gambling
- vocational services, including training in assistive technology, vocational counseling and training, educational counseling, job-retention assistance, hearing evaluations, and computer training to help people who are deaf or hearing impaired seek and maintain employment.

ELIGIBILITY CRITERIA
Eligibility criteria vary depending on the nature of the services provided, consumers' needs, the treatment provider, available health insurance coverage, and funding sources.

CONTACT INFORMATION
Contact private and public agencies at the state and local levels that provide assistance to people who are deaf or hearing impaired. Examples of such agencies include state and county agencies for people who are deaf or hearing impaired, and diverse nonprofit agencies.

Services for People with HIV/AIDS

SERVICES AND BENEFITS
A wide variety of public and private programs provide services to people who are HIV positive or who have AIDS. Typical services include

- burial assistance
- diagnosis and testing
- financial assistance, information, and referral
- HIV/AIDS prevention
- home health care and homemaking assistance
- housing assistance
- medical treatment for opportunistic infections, dementia, wasting syndrome, nephropathy, malignancies, lymphoma, and Kaposi's sarcoma
- mental health treatment
- nutrition and exercise
- substance abuse treatment.

Eligibility criteria vary depending on the nature of the services provided, consumers' needs, the treatment provider, available health insurance coverage, and funding sources.

Contact public and private agencies at the state and local levels that provide assistance to people who are HIV positive or who have AIDS. Examples of such agencies include departments of health, hospitals, health clinics, and specialty HIV/AIDS clinics.

Hospice and Palliative Care

Services and Benefits
Services include hospice and palliative care. Hospice services provide comfort and support to patients and their families when life-limiting illness no longer responds to medical treatment. Typical hospice programs provide physician and nursing services; home health aides; medical appliances and supplies; mental health, spiritual, and dietary counseling; and bereavement services. Palliative care includes treatment designed to relieve distressing pain and symptoms, provide comfort, and enhance the quality of life during the last phase of life. Palliative care does not address underlying disease.

Eligibility Criteria
Eligibility criteria vary depending on the nature of the services provided, consumers' needs, the treatment provider, available health insurance coverage, and funding sources. Most people who use hospice and palliative care are elderly and are entitled to services offered by the Medicare hospice benefit. Most private health insurance plans and state-sponsored Medicaid programs cover hospice services.

Contact Information
Contact local agencies, such as specialty hospice programs, visiting nurses, hospitals, area offices on aging, community health clinics, and senior centers for information about hospice and palliative care programs. The

National Association of Professional Geriatric Care Managers helps people locate a professional care manager (http://www.caremanager.org/).

Health Insurance

Health insurance takes many forms. Many private and public organizations and sponsors offer plans that cover health care, disability, and special needs.

- Private Health Insurance. For many workers, health care coverage is provided as an employee benefit through direct payment of premiums to private health insurance companies. Some employers offer only one health plan; others allow employees to choose from among several options, such as fee-for-service plans, a health maintenance organization (HMO), or a preferred provider organization (PPO). Employees who leave a job and lose health care benefits may be entitled under the federal Consolidated Omnibus Reconciliation Act (COBRA) to continue their coverage for a limited period by paying a special premium. Coverage and benefits, such as doctors' visits, hospital care, and home health care, vary among different health insurance plans. Group health and individual insurance plans are available. A number of companies market "retail" supplemental health care plans and/or specialized plans for dental or vision care.
- Medicare. Medicare is the federal health insurance program for people age 65 and older and for people younger than age 65 who have certain disabilities. Medicare covers hospital-based care under Part A and covers physicians' and other health-related services under Part B. Additional premiums paid by covered individuals are required for coverage under Part B. Part C is the combination of Part A and Part B. The main difference in Part C is that it is provided through private insurance companies approved by Medicare. Part D is stand-alone prescription drug coverage insurance. Most people do have to pay a premium for this coverage. Plans vary and cover different drugs, but all medically necessary drugs are covered.
- Medicaid. Medicaid is a federal program, operated by the states, that provides health care coverage for low-income people. Medicaid

provides health care services for people who are elderly, blind, or disabled, and for certain people in families with disabled children. Each state determines its own eligibility criteria for Medicaid and what services the program will cover in that state.

- Private Disability Insurance. Some employers offer group disability insurance as a separate benefit from health insurance. Individuals also can purchase disability insurance coverage through private insurance companies.
- Hospital Indemnity Insurance. This type of insurance pays covered policyholders a specific amount of money for each day of a hospital stay up to a maximum number of days. Unlike other types of health insurance, hospital indemnity insurance provides funds that the covered individual may apply to general expenses, such as paying household bills, and not only to health care–related expenses.
- Long-Term Care Insurance. This type of insurance, offered by private companies, professional and business associations, and consumer interest groups, specifically covers the cost of nursing home care.

ELIGIBILITY CRITERIA

Insurance providers have diverse eligibility criteria that may include health care status, employment status, and income.

CONTACT INFORMATION

Contact local offices of the Social Security Administration, state or county human services and health departments, and private insurers for information about various insurance plans.

Pharmaceutical Assistance

SERVICES AND BENEFITS

Many states sponsor programs that provide some form of pharmaceutical coverage or assistance, primarily to low-income elderly people or people with disabilities who do not qualify for Medicaid. Medicare beneficiaries may apply for and use one of a number of different Medicare discount programs endorsed by HHS. Some programs, such as the AIDS Drug

Assistance Program (ADAP) funded by the Ryan White Care Act, provide pharmaceutical assistance to specific patient populations.

ELIGIBILITY CRITERIA
Eligibility criteria vary according to different state and federal program requirements. Eligibility ordinarily is based on age, disability, and income. Some state programs are subsidized with state funds, and some offer consumers state-negotiated discounts.

CONTACT INFORMATION
Contact the state agency that administers the pharmaceutical assistance program and Medicaid program. For information about pharmaceutical discounts under the Medicare program, contact local offices of the Social Security Administration, area offices on aging, departments of elderly affairs, health departments, HIV/AIDS programs, and senior centers.

Legal Options and Assistance

SERVICES AND BENEFITS
People may execute several legal options with regard to their health care. The most important of these legal options concern advance directives, durable powers of attorney, and living wills.

- Advance Directives. An advance directive is a written statement that expresses what procedures or treatments an individual does or does not want if, in the future, he or she cannot express his or her wishes about medical treatment.
- Durable Power of Attorney for Health Care. A durable power of attorney for health care is a document that gives another person, chosen by the patient, the right to act on the patient's behalf in making medical decisions in the event that the patient is unable to participate in such decisions.
- Living Will. A living will is an individual's written and witnessed declaration that expresses his or her wishes about the use or withdrawal of life-sustaining procedures in the event that the individual loses the capacity to decide for himself or herself and when such procedures would merely prolong dying.

ELIGIBILITY CRITERIA

All competent people can create advance directives, durable powers of attorney for health care, and living wills.

CONTACT INFORMATION

Private attorneys and legal aid clinics can provide legal assistance to people who are seeking to create advance directives, durable powers of attorney for health care, or living wills. Referrals can be obtained from local bar associations and legal aid societies and clinics that provide assistance to low-income people.

Medical Information

SERVICES AND BENEFITS

Consumers can obtain basic information about illnesses and diseases from a variety of health care books, encyclopedias, and publications. In addition, prominent health care and human services organizations also sponsor comprehensive Web sites that can provide valuable information. Examples include

- Centers for Disease Control and Prevention (http://www.cdc.gov/)
- ClinicalTrials.gov, sponsored by the National Institutes of Health (NIH) (http://clinicaltrials.gov/)
- Medline Plus, sponsored by the U.S. National Library of Medicine and NIH (http://medlineplus.gov/)
- healthfinder, an interactive site offered by the National Health Information Center at HHS (http://www.healthfinder.gov/)
- Health Information, sponsored by NIH (http://health.nih.gov/)

Useful Tips

Additional information about important health care topics is available from a variety of organizational Web sites. Consult the following topical Web sites:

- Adult day care
  - o National Adult Day Services Association (http://www.nadsa.org/)

- Alzheimer's disease
  - o Alzheimer's Association (http://www.alz.org/)
  - o MedlinePlus, NIH (http://www.nlm.nih.gov/medlineplus/alzheimersdisease.html)
- Assisted living
  - o Assisted Living Federation of America (http://www.alfa.org/)
  - o Medline Plus, NIH (http://www.nlm.nih.gov/medlineplus/assistedliving.html)
- Cancer
  - o American Cancer Society (http://www.cancer.org/)
  - o MedlinePlus, NIH (http://www.nlm.nih.gov/medlineplus/cancer.html)
- Developmental disability
  - o Administration on Developmental Disabilities, Administration for Children and Families, HHS (http://www.acf.hhs.gov/programs/add/)
  - o MedlinePlus, NIH (http://www.nlm.nih.gov/medlineplus/developmentaldisabilities.html)
  - o National Association of Councils on Developmental Disabilities (http://www.nacdd.org/)
- Diabetes
  - o American Diabetes Association (http://www.diabetes.org/)
  - o MedlinePlus, NIH (http://www.nlm.nih.gov/medlineplus/diabetes.html)
- Disability
  - o MedlinePlus, NIH (http://www.nlm.nih.gov/medlineplus/disabilities.html)
  - o U.S. Government, Disability Information Web site (http://www.disabilityinfo.gov)
- Heart disease
  - o American Heart Association (http://www.americanheart.org/)
  - o MedlinePlus, NIH (http://www.nlm.nih.gov/medlineplus/heartdiseases.html)
  - o National Heart, Lung and Blood Institute (http://www.nhlbi.nih.gov/)

- HIV and AIDS
  - o AIDS information, HHS (http://www.aidsinfo.nih.gov/)
  - o HIV/AIDS Bureau, Health Resources and Services Administration, HHS (http://hab.hrsa.gov/)
  - o MedlinePlus, NIH (http://www.nlm.nih.gov/medlineplus/aids.html)
- Home care
  - o Medline Plus, NIH (http://www.nlm.nih.gov/medlineplus/homecareservices.html)
  - o National Association for Home Care and Hospice (http://www.nahc.org/)
- Hospice
  - o Hospice Foundation of America (http://www.hospicefoundation.org/)
  - o MedlinePlus, NIH (http://www.nlm.nih.gov/medlineplus/hospicecare.html)
  - o National Association for Home Care and Hospice (http://www.nahc.org/)
  - o National Hospice and Palliative Care Organization (http://www.nhpco.org)
- Lung disease
  - o American Lung Association (http://www.lungusa.org/)
  - o MedlinePlus, NIH(http://www.nlm.nih.gov/medlineplus/lungdiseases.html)
  - o National Heart, Lung and Blood Institute (http://www.nhlbi.nih.gov/)
- Maternal and child health
  - o Maternal and Child Health Bureau, Health Resources and Services Administration, HHS (http://mchb.hrsa.gov)
- Medicare and Medicaid
  - o Centers for Medicare and Medicaid Services (CMS), HHS (http://www.cms.hhs.gov/)
  - o MedlinePlus, NIH (http://www.nlm.nih.gov/medlineplus/medicaid.html and http://www.nlm.nih.gov/medlineplus/medicare.html)

- Nursing homes
  - o CMS, HHS (http://www.medicare.gov/Nursing/Overview.asp)
  - o MedlinePlus, NIH (http://www.nlm.nih.gov/medlineplus/ nursinghomes.html)
  - o Nursing Home Compare (http://www.medicare.gov/NH Compare/Include/DataSection/Questions/SearchCriteria.asp? version=default&browser=IE%7C6%7CWinXP&language= English&defaultstatus=0&pagelist=Home)
- Nutrition
  - o Food and Nutrition Information Center, U.S. Department of Agriculture (USDA) (http://www.nutrition.gov/)
  - o Food and Nutrition Service, USDA (http://www.fns.usda.govfns/)
  - o MedlinePlus, NIH (http://www.nlm.nih.gov/medlineplus/ nutrition.html)
- Rehabilitation
  - o Medline Plus, NIH (http://www.nlm.nih.gov/medlineplus/ rehabilitation.html)
  - o National Rehabilitation Association (http://www.national rehab.org)
  - o National Rehabilitation Information Center (http://www. naric.com/)
- Reproductive health
  - o Association of Reproductive Health Professionals (http://www. arhp.org/)
  - o MedlinePlus, NIH (http://www.nlm.nih.gov/medlineplus/ reproductivehealth.html)
  - o Centers for Disease Control and Prevention, HHS (http:// www.cdc.gov/reproductivehealth/)
- Services for the blind and visually impaired
  - o American Foundation for the Blind (http://www.afb.org/)
  - o American Council of the Blind (http://www.acb.org)
  - o MedlinePlus, NIH (http://www.nlm.nih.gov/medlineplus/ visionimpairmentandblindness.html)
  - o National Library Service for the Blind and Physically Handicapped (http://www.loc.gov/nls/)

- Services for the deaf and hearing impaired
  o MedlinePlus, NIH (http://www.nlm.nih.gov/medlineplus/hearingdisordersanddeafness.html)
  o National Association for the Deaf (http://www.nad.org/)

MENTAL HEALTH SERVICES

Overview

IN MANY PEOPLE'S lives, times arise in which they feel the need for help with a personal crisis or chronic struggle. People may seek help with marital conflict, problems in relationships, suicidal feelings, depression, loneliness, coping with physical disability, or other troubling issues.

A wide variety of professionals and agencies offer mental health services. In most communities counseling and mental health services are available from

- clinical social workers, who hold master's or doctoral degrees and receive training in a variety of perspectives on mental health and counseling approaches
- clinical and counseling psychologists, who have master's or doctoral degrees and receive training in a variety of perspectives on mental health and counseling approaches
- mental health counselors, who typically have master's degrees and receive training in a variety of perspectives on mental health and counseling approaches
- marriage and family therapists, who typically have master's degrees and receive training in a variety of perspectives on mental health and counseling approaches focusing on couples and families

- addictions counselors (alcohol, drugs, gambling), who typically are certified or licensed and may or may not have graduate-level education in a counseling or mental health profession
- pastoral counselors, who are certified mental health professionals who use spiritual resources as well as psychological and mental health theories and interventions to help people in need
- psychiatric nurses, who have nursing (RN) degrees, receive training in a variety of perspectives on mental health and counseling approaches, and may have additional graduate-level training in the mental health field that allows them to prescribe medications
- psychiatrists, who are medical doctors who may provide counseling services and can prescribe psychotropic and neuroleptic medications that help people with symptoms of disorders such as depression, anxiety, bipolar illness, schizophrenia, and impulse control.

Community-Based Counseling and Psychotherapy

SERVICES AND BENEFITS

Community-based counseling and psychotherapy services are delivered in a variety of ways and in a variety of settings. The most common sources and settings are

- community mental health centers
- family service agencies
- hospital psychiatry and outpatient clinics
- home-based counseling services
- Internet counseling
- private counseling offices.

Community mental health centers offer a wide range of mental health services to adults and children. Most centers provide crisis intervention services and individual, family, couples, and group counseling. Many community health centers sponsor support groups for people with mental illness.

Family service agencies also offer a wide range of mental health services to adults and children. Most agencies provide individual, family, couples, and group counseling. Some agencies sponsor support groups for people with mental illness.

Many psychiatric and general medical hospitals sponsor outpatient clinics for people who struggle with mental illness. Some agencies provide home-based counseling services to individuals and families in need. Often these services focus on crisis situations. A number of Web-based counseling services are available to people who do not live near mental health programs and agencies or who do not want to receive in-person counseling. (This nontraditional form of counseling is somewhat controversial and has not been regulated to the same extent as licensed and accredited mental health programs.) Traditional forms of counseling also are available in private offices from clinical social workers, psychologists, psychiatrists, counselors, psychiatric nurses, and pastoral counselors.

ELIGIBILITY CRITERIA
Eligibility criteria for mental health services may vary depending on mental health needs, clinical diagnosis, age, community of residence, and insurance coverage.

CONTACT INFORMATION
Contact community mental health centers, family service agencies, hospital psychiatry and outpatient clinics, private counselors, clergy, and other organizations and professionals familiar with local mental health resources.

Home-Based Family Intervention

SERVICES AND BENEFITS
Many social service agencies provide home-based intervention for families in crisis or in need of supportive services. Home-based intervention is an intensive type of mental health counseling designed to help stabilize difficult family situations so that children can continue to live at home and families can remain intact. Typical services include intensive clinical and family support services, such as family therapy; case management; referrals to other community agencies; and advocacy in schools, courts, residential treatment programs, and psychiatric hospitals.

ELIGIBILITY CRITERIA

Eligibility criteria for home-based family intervention services may vary depending on family members' mental health needs and risk factors, community of residence, and program funding.

CONTACT INFORMATION

Contact community mental health centers, family service agencies, hospital psychiatry and outpatient clinics, private counselors, and other organizations and professionals familiar with local mental health resources.

Emergency Mental Health Services and Crisis Intervention

SERVICES AND BENEFITS

Emergency mental health and crisis intervention services may be available from community mental health centers, psychiatric hospitals, and hospital emergency rooms.

ELIGIBILITY CRITERIA

Eligibility for emergency mental health and crisis intervention services may depend on mental health needs, clinical diagnosis, age, community of residence, and insurance coverage. Some mental health and health care agencies, such as hospital emergency rooms and community mental health centers, may provide emergency services regardless of ability to pay.

CONTACT INFORMATION

Contact community mental health centers, hospital emergency rooms, family service agencies, hospital psychiatry and outpatient clinics, private counselors, clergy, police, rescue professionals, and other organizations and professionals familiar with local mental health resources.

Intellectual Disability

SERVICES AND BENEFITS

A variety of public and private agencies provide community-based and residential services for people with intellectual disabilities. Services typically include residential care, counseling, adult day programs, training for independent living, home health care, attendant care, case management, employment support, education, transportation, and respite care.

ELIGIBILITY CRITERIA
Eligibility for services for people with intellectual disabilities depends on various criteria, such as the extent of a person's disability, his or her need for social supports, age, community of residence, and insurance coverage.

CONTACT INFORMATION
Contact the local division or office of intellectual disabilities (in some locations known as the division or office of mental retardation) and voluntary organizations, such as The Arc.

Residential Care

SERVICES AND BENEFITS
Residential mental health services that assist people with psychiatric challenges and intellectual disabilities are available in several settings. Residential services may be offered through public or private agencies. The most common providers of residential services are

- psychiatric hospitals and psychiatric units in general medical hospitals that offer inpatient mental health services
- supervised group homes and residential programs, which are sponsored by public or private mental health agencies to provide residential care and social services for people with chronic mental illness and intellectual disabilities.

ELIGIBILITY CRITERIA
Eligibility for residential mental health services depends on various criteria, such as mental health needs, clinical diagnosis, age, community of residence, and insurance coverage.

CONTACT INFORMATION
Contact community mental health centers, family service agencies, hospital psychiatry and outpatient clinics, private counselors, and other organizations and professionals familiar with local mental health resources.

Support Groups

Services and Benefits

Many communities offer general and specialized support groups for people with mental illness or intellectual disabilities and their families. General support groups assist people who are coping with mental illness and intellectual disabilities. Specialized support groups focus on specific disabilities and address issues such as anxiety, depression, schizophrenia, eating disorders, bipolar disorder, crime victimization, sexual trauma and abuse, cancer, and infertility.

Eligibility Criteria

Participation in support groups ordinarily is based on self-selection or referral by professionals in therapeutic programs.

Contact Information

Contact community mental health centers, family service agencies, hospital psychiatry and outpatient clinics, private counselors, clergy, and other organizations and professionals familiar with local mental health resources.

Bereavement Services

Services and Benefits

Many mental health agencies and practitioners offer bereavement services to people who are struggling with the death of a loved one. Bereavement or grief counseling provides assistance and support to people who experience emotional and psychological stress after the death of a loved one. Trained counselors specialize in treatment of grief and loss.

Eligibility Criteria

Eligibility criteria for bereavement and grief counseling may vary depending on mental health needs, clinical diagnosis, and insurance coverage.

Contact Information

Contact community mental health centers, family service agencies, hospital psychiatry and outpatient clinics, private mental health and pastoral counselors, clergy, and other organizations and professionals familiar with local bereavement and grief counseling resources.

Useful Tips

Several national organizations make available valuable information about mental health, mental health services, developmental and intellectual disabilities, policies, and education. Consult the Web sites of organizations such as

- the American Association of Suicidology, which promotes research, public awareness programs, education, and training related to suicide and the membership of which includes mental health and public health professionals, suicide prevention and crisis intervention centers and professionals, survivors of suicide attempts, and other people who have an interest in suicide prevention (www.suicidology.org)
- the American Association on Intellectual and Developmental Disabilities, which promotes policy, research, education, and advocacy on behalf of people with intellectual disabilities (www.aamr.org)
- the American Academy of Grief Counseling (http://www.aihcp. org/aagc.htm)
- the Bazelon Center for Mental Health Law, which specializes in legal advocacy for people with mental disabilities and uses its legal expertise to address institutional abuse and violations of consumers' rights (www.bazelon.org)
- the National Alliance for the Mentally Ill, a nonprofit grassroots self-help support and advocacy organization of consumers, families, and friends of people with severe mental illnesses, such as schizophrenia, bipolar disorder, major depressive disorder, obsessive–compulsive disorder, panic disorder, anxiety disorder, attention-deficit/hyperactivity disorder, autism, and pervasive developmental disorder (www.nami.org)
- the National Institute of Mental Health, which is part of the National Institutes of Health, U.S. Department of Health and Human Services, and which provides a comprehensive Web site with clinical

and research-related information about all forms of mental illness (http://www.nimh.nih.gov/)
- the National Mental Health Association, a nonprofit organization that addresses all aspects of mental health and mental illness and works to improve and promote mental health through advocacy, education, research, and service (www.nmha.org).

Several national organizations also make Web sites available for consumers of mental health services. Important examples include

- Mental Health America, an organization that provides referrals to a broad range of local services and support groups, as well as literature on various mental health issues (http://www.nmha.org/infoctr/index.cfm)
- The Arc, a chapter-based organization that serves people with intellectual and developmental disabilities and their families, provides supportive services, and promotes education and policies related to mental retardation (http://www.thearc.org)
- The Bright Side, which aims to provide support to anyone who is feeling emotionally overwhelmed by offering a volunteer-facilitated online community and providing information and support (http://www.the-bright-side.org)
- the Child and Adolescent Bipolar Foundation, a parent-led organization that educates parents, families, and the public about pediatric bipolar disorder; connects families with resources; advocates for and empowers families; and supports research on pediatric bipolar disorder (http://www.bpkids.org/)
- Compeer, which matches community volunteers in supportive friendships with children and adults who are receiving mental health treatment; activities include going to movies, shopping, playing sports, having coffee, and participating in other activities (http://www.compeer.org)
- the Depression and Bipolar Support Alliance, a consumer-directed organization that sponsors support groups, advocacy, and educational efforts related to depression and bipolar disorder (http://www.dbsalliance.org)

- the Eating Disorder Referral and Information Center, which provides information and treatment resources for all forms of eating disorders, such as anorexia nervosa, bulimia nervosa, and binge eating (http://www.edreferral.com)
- Families for Depression Awareness, which helps families recognize and cope with depressive disorders; provides education, advocacy, and support to families and friends; and is made up of families who have lost a family member to suicide or have watched a family member struggle with depression (http://www.familyaware.org)
- the Federation of Families for Children's Mental Health, a family-run organization that provides education and advocacy concerning the mental health needs of children and their families (http://www.ffcmh.org)
- Freedom From Fear, a mental health organization that provides information and education to people who are coping with severe anxiety or depression (http://www.freedomfromfear.org)
- the National Coalition of Mental Health Professionals and Consumers, which includes consumers, professionals, and consumer advocates who promote reforms in the mental health field, focusing especially on issues related to managed care and the regulation of mental health treatment (www.thenationalcoalition.org)
- the National Family Caregivers Association, a grassroots association that provides education, support, and advocacy for people who provide care for someone with a chronic disability (http://www.nfcacares.org/)
- the National Mental Health Consumers' Self-Help Clearinghouse, a consumer-run technical assistance center serving the mental health consumer movement that connects people to self-help and advocacy resources and assists self-help groups and other peer-run services for mental health consumers (http://www.mhselfhelp.org/)
- the International Obsessive–Compulsive Foundation, which is composed of people with obsessive–compulsive disorder (or related disorders), their families, friends, and professionals and provides education, support, and advocacy services (http://www.ocfoundation.org/)

Many professional associations concerned with mental health services and mental illness also provide information useful to consumers. Some notable examples include

- the National Association of Social Workers (http://www.helpstartshere.org/)
- the American Association of Pastoral Counselors (http://www.aapc.org/)
- the American Counseling Association (http://www.counseling.org)
- the American Psychiatric Association (http://www.psych.org)
- the American Psychiatric Nurses Association (http://www.apna.org)
- the American Psychological Association (http://www.apa.org)
- the Association for Addiction Professionals (http://www.naadac.org/)

ADDICTIONS

Overview

MANY PEOPLE STRUGGLE with addictions. Addiction is the compulsive use of a substance or activity that leads to physical, psychological, or social harm to the user. Some people seek help at the first signs of their addiction, whereas others seek help only after many years of problems associated with their addictions, such as marital, parenting, job, legal, and financial difficulties.

Addictions tend to come in clusters; many people have more than one addiction. The most common addictions involve

- alcohol
- drugs
- food
- gambling
- the Internet and computer use
- nicotine
- sex
- spending or shopping.

Alcoholism occurs when a person is physically or psychologically dependent on alcohol consumption. Alcohol abuse entails consumption of alcohol in such a way as to harm or endanger the well-being of the user or people with whom the user comes in contact. Such consumption often leads the abuser to cause accidents, become physically assaultive and less productive, or deteriorate physically. Alcohol dependence includes a daily need or wish for alcohol, inconsistent attempts to control drinking, physical disorders aggravated by use of alcohol, occasional binges, absences or ineffectiveness at work, violence, and problems in social relationships.

Drug addiction involves the abuse of chemical substances, such as amphetamines, cannabis, cocaine, hallucinogens, opium, and sedatives, that results in a physiological dependence in which the body tissues require the substance to function comfortably. Drug abuse includes the inappropriate use of a chemical substance in ways that are detrimental to the user's physical or mental well-being. Drug dependence includes the misuse and reliance on chemical substances; continued use; craving; and other cognitive, behavioral, and physiological symptoms that occur through the use of drugs. Typical symptoms of drug addiction include being preoccupied with the substance; taking greater amounts than intended; making persistent efforts to control the use of the substance; reducing occupational or social activities; and continually using the substance despite recognizing that it is causing recurrent physical, psychological, or social problems.

Food addiction occurs when people have difficulty controlling their eating, think obsessively about food, and experience social or other difficulties as a result of the way they eat. Common symptoms of food addiction include feeling obsessed with food, feeling a loss of control when eating, repeated use of food to create a sense of comfort, being preoccupied with finding sources of food associated with pleasure and comfort, engaging in a cycle of binge eating despite intellectual understanding of the negative consequences, eating much more quickly than usual, sneaking food, eating until uncomfortably full, eating when not hungry, eating sensibly in front of others but overeating when alone, guilt or shame after eating, and having a physical craving for food that overrides one's judgment.

Gambling addiction is a behavior disorder in which a person becomes preoccupied with wagers and betting and develops a progressively worsening urge to bet money. The person also may relive past gambling experiences, plan the next venture, and think of ways to get money to gamble. A person who is addicted to gambling may need to gamble with increasing amounts of money to achieve the desired excitement; repeatedly try, without success, to stop gambling; become restless or irritable when attempting to stop gambling; gamble as a way of escaping problems or relieving a sense of helplessness, guilt, anxiety, or depression; return to gambling after losing money in order to "get even"; lie to family members, counselors, and others to conceal the extent of his or her gambling; commit illegal acts such as fraud, forgery, theft, or embezzlement to finance gambling; jeopardize or lose a significant relationship, job, educational or career opportunity because of gambling; and rely on others to provide money or to relieve a desperate financial situation caused by gambling. The urge to gamble often becomes uncontrollable and occurs even when funds for making bets are unavailable.

Addiction to the computer and the Internet involves the compulsive misuse of this technology. Common symptoms include a continuous preoccupation with computers, the Internet, or both; anxiety, depression, restlessness, and irritability when not engaged in computer activities; the need to spend increasing time on computers to change moods; neglecting obligations; lying to others about the amount of time spent on computer activities; losing relationships and opportunities because of computer activity; inability to control computer activities; a decline in physical well-being; and continued use of the computer despite experiencing personal problems because of its use.

Nicotine addiction is a psychoactive substance abuse disorder that involves inhaling the smoke of burning tobacco or ingesting chewed tobacco. Nicotine-related disorders can develop with use of cigarettes, chewing tobacco, snuff, cigars, and pipes. Common symptoms of nicotine addiction include depression, insomnia, irritability, anxiety, and difficulty concentrating.

Sex addiction involves a compulsive craving for sexual intercourse or stimulation, usually accompanied by extreme interpersonal dependence; preoccupation with romantic fantasies; inability to achieve or maintain true intimacy; and behavior that is ultimately demeaning and unacceptable.

Addictive or compulsive spending and shopping occur when a person feels a compelling need to spend money and purchase items. Common symptoms include spending or shopping as a result of being disappointed, angry, or scared; spending and shopping habits that cause emotional distress and chaos in a person's life; having arguments with others because of spending and shopping habits; feeling lost without credit cards; buying items on credits cards that would not be bought with cash; experiencing a rush of euphoria and anxiety when spending money; feeling that spending and shopping are a reckless or forbidden activity; feeling guilty, ashamed, embarrassed, or confused after spending money or shopping; and purchasing items that are never used. A person with a spending and shopping addiction also may lie to others about what he or she has bought or how much was spent, think excessively about money, and devote a lot of time to juggling credit card and bank accounts to accommodate spending.

Alcoholism

Services and Benefits
Treatment for alcoholism is available from a variety of service providers and in a variety of settings. Residential treatment settings include detoxification programs, independent rehabilitation programs, hospital inpatient programs, halfway houses, 3/4-way houses, and sober houses. Community-based and outpatient treatment programs include partial hospitalization or day treatment, counseling, and 12-step meetings.

Detoxification programs provide medically monitored care of people who are having acute problems resulting from withdrawal from alcohol use. Typical services include physical examination; nursing evaluation; biopsychosocial assessment; monitoring for withdrawal complications, such as elevated vital signs, tremors, sweats, or seizures; medical treatment and hospital care; special diets; individual and group counseling; family involvement; and discharge planning.

Independent rehabilitation programs typically offer individual and group counseling, educational sessions, practice in recovery and relapse prevention skills, an introduction to Alcoholics Anonymous (AA), discharge planning, and family educational and counseling sessions. Programs may be short term (30 days or less) or long term (more than 30 days).

Hospital inpatient services for people with alcohol addiction include individual and group counseling, educational sessions, practice in recovery and relapse prevention skills, an introduction to AA, discharge planning, and family educational and counseling sessions. Inpatient services may be short term (30 days or less) or long term (more than 30 days).

Halfway houses and 3/4-way houses provide structured, community-based settings for people receiving treatment and counseling for alcoholism. Halfway houses provide more structure and supervision than do 3/4-way houses. Typical services include individual and group counseling, educational sessions, practice in recovery and relapse prevention skills, an introduction to AA, discharge planning, and family educational and counseling sessions. Programs may be short term (30 days or less) or long term (more than 30 days).

Sober houses provide a group-living environment with peer support for people who are actively involved in recovery. Sober houses do not provide formal treatment. These facilities usually require residents to work, attend 12-step and support meetings, and remain alcohol free. Sober houses are sometimes called rehab homes, boarding homes, hostels, shelters, recovery support homes, or sober shelters.

Community-based and outpatient programs available to assist people with an alcohol addiction include partial hospitalization or day treatment, counseling, and 12-step meetings.

Partial hospitalization or day treatment programs provide intensive structure for people receiving treatment who are able to return to a safe home or other setting at the end of the day. Consumers typically arrive in the morning and participate in an extensive recovery program throughout the day, possibly extending into the evening. Common services include individual and group counseling, educational sessions, practice in recovery and relapse prevention skills, an introduction to AA, discharge planning; and family educational and counseling sessions.

Counseling services are available from community mental health centers, family service agencies, community action programs, independent alcoholism treatment programs, psychiatric hospitals, general hospitals, and private counselors and psychotherapists. Common services include individual and group counseling, educational sessions, practice in recovery and relapse prevention skills, an introduction to AA, discharge planning, and family educational and counseling sessions.

The most well-known 12-step group is AA, a voluntary fellowship of men and women who share their experiences with one another in an effort to attain and maintain sobriety. AA is a program of total abstinence. Sobriety is maintained through sharing experiences at group meetings and through the program's 12 steps for recovery from alcoholism.

Specialized services and programs also are available in many communities to address the special needs of adolescents with alcohol addiction; people with co-occurring disorders, such as alcoholism and mental illness; people with HIV/AIDS; people who are gay, lesbian, bisexual, or transgender; elderly people; pregnant or postpartum women; people convicted of driving under the influence of alcohol or driving while intoxicated; criminal justice clients; health care and other professionals; women; and men.

ELIGIBILITY CRITERIA

Eligibility for services is based on each program's intake criteria. Such criteria may include evidence of alcoholism, treatment history, insurance coverage, and ability to pay. Funding sources include private health insurance, Medicaid, Medicare, military insurance, and self-payment. For AA the only requirement for membership is a desire to stop drinking.

CONTACT INFORMATION

Contact state and local government-sponsored substance abuse departments, public and private-sector substance abuse treatment programs, health departments, community mental health agencies, family service agencies, community action programs, hospital social service departments, clergy, and local contacts for AA.

Drug Abuse

SERVICES AND BENEFITS

A variety of service providers offer treatment for drug abuse in a variety of settings. Residential treatment settings include detoxification programs, independent rehabilitation programs, hospital inpatient programs, half-way houses, and 3/4-way houses. Community-based and outpatient programs for people with drug addictions include methadone maintenance programs, partial hospitalization or day treatments, counseling, 12-step meetings, and "drug court."

Detoxification programs provide medically monitored care of people who are having acute problems resulting from withdrawal from drug use. Typical services include a physical examinations; a nursing evaluation; biopsychosocial assessment; monitoring for withdrawal complications, such as elevated vital signs, tremors, sweats, or seizures; medical treatment and hospital care; special diets; individual and group counseling; family involvement; and discharge planning.

Independent rehabilitation programs typically offer individual and group counseling; educational sessions; practice in recovery and relapse prevention skills; an introduction to Narcotics Anonymous (NA), Cocaine Anonymous (CA), and Methadone Anonymous (MA); discharge planning; and family educational and counseling sessions. Programs may be short term (30 days or less) or long term (more than 30 days).

Hospital inpatient services typically include individual and group counseling; educational sessions; practice in recovery and relapse prevention skills; an introduction to NA, CA, and MA; discharge planning; and family educational and counseling sessions. Hospital stays may be short term (30 days or less) or long term (more than 30 days).

Halfway houses and 3/4-way houses provide a structured, community-based setting for people receiving treatment and counseling for drug abuse. Halfway houses provide more structure and supervision than do 3/4-way houses. Typical services include individual and group counseling; educational sessions; practice in recovery and relapse prevention skills; an introduction to NA, CA, and MA; discharge planning; and family educational and counseling sessions. Residential services may be short term (30 days or less) or long term (more than 30 days).

Methadone maintenance programs were created to assist people addicted to heroin. Methadone is a long-acting opioid drug that prevents withdrawal, reduces drug cravings, and blocks the euphoric effects of heroin and other opioids. Typical methadone maintenance programs provide assessment; methadone dosing; analysis and review of urine screen results; administration of home-based services; communication with other service providers; substance abuse counseling; pain management; general health care; screening, treatment, and referral for infectious diseases, such as HIV, hepatitis, sexually transmitted diseases, or tuberculosis; and vocational services.

Partial hospitalization or day treatment programs provide intensive structure for people receiving treatment who are able to return to a safe home or other environment at the end of the day. Consumers typically arrive in the morning and participate in an extensive recovery program throughout the day, possibly extending into the evening. Common services include individual and group counseling; educational sessions; practice in recovery and relapse prevention skills; an introduction to NA, CA, and MA; discharge planning; and family educational and counseling sessions.

Counseling services are available from community mental health centers, family service agencies, community action programs, independent treatment programs, psychiatric hospitals, general hospitals, and private counselors and psychotherapists. Common services include individual and group counseling; educational sessions; practice in recovery and relapse prevention skills; an introduction to NA, CA, and MA; discharge planning; and family educational and counseling sessions.

The most common 12-step groups that address drug addictions are NA, CA, and MA. NA, CA, and MA, like AA, are voluntary fellowships of men and women who share their experiences with one another in an effort to attain and maintain abstinence. Abstinence is maintained through sharing experiences at group meetings and through the programs' 12 steps and 12 traditions for recovery from drug abuse.

A drug court is a special court given the responsibility to handle substance-abusing criminal offenders through comprehensive supervision; drug testing; treatment services; sanctions; and incentives, such as avoiding jail and prison. Plans for offenders are developed by judges, prosecutors, defense counsel, substance abuse treatment professionals, social workers, probation officers, law enforcement and corrections officials, educational and vocational personnel, community leaders, and others.

Specialized services and programs also are available in many communities for adolescents; people with co-occurring disorders, such as mental illness; people with HIV/AIDS; people who are gay, lesbian, bisexual, or transgender; elderly people; pregnant or postpartum women; people convicted of driving under the influence; criminal justice clients; health care and other professionals; women; and men.

ELIGIBILITY CRITERIA

Eligibility for services is based on each program's intake criteria. Such criteria may include evidence of drug abuse, treatment history, insurance coverage, and ability to pay. Funding sources include private health insurance, Medicaid, Medicare, military insurance, and self-payment. Membership in NA, CA, and MA is available to all substance abusers.

CONTACT INFORMATION

Contact state and local government-sponsored substance abuse agencies, local health departments, public- and private-sector substance abuse treatment programs, community mental health agencies, family service agencies, community action programs, hospital social service departments, public defenders' offices, court personnel, clergy, and the local contacts for NA, CA, and MA.

Gambling

SERVICES AND BENEFITS

A variety of service providers offer treatment for gambling addiction in a variety of settings. Residential treatment settings include independent rehabilitation programs, hospital inpatient programs, halfway houses, 3/4-way houses, and sober houses. Community-based and outpatient treatment programs include partial hospitalization and day treatment programs, counseling, and 12-step meetings.

Independent rehabilitation programs typically offer individual and group counseling, educational sessions, practice in recovery and relapse prevention skills, an introduction to Gamblers Anonymous (GA), discharge planning, and family educational and counseling sessions. Residential services may be short term (30 days or less) or long term (more than 30 days).

Hospital inpatient services typically include individual and group counseling, educational sessions, practice in recovery and relapse prevention skills, introduction to GA, discharge planning, and family educational and counseling sessions. Residential services may be short term (30 days or less) or long term (more than 30 days).

A halfway house or a 3/4-way house can provide a structured, community-based setting for people receiving treatment and counseling for compulsive gambling. Halfway houses provide more structure and supervision than do 3/4-way houses. Typical services include individual and group counseling, educational sessions, practice in recovery and relapse prevention skills, introduction to GA, discharge planning, and family educational and counseling sessions. Residential services may be short term (30 days or less) or long term (more than 30 days).

Sober houses provide a group-living environment with peer support for people who are actively involved in recovery. Some sober houses provide services to people with gambling addictions. Sober houses do not provide formal treatment. These facilities usually require residents to work, attend 12-step and support meetings, and not gamble. Sober houses also may be referred to as rehab homes, boarding homes, hostels, shelters, recovery support homes, or sober shelters.

Partial hospitalization and day treatment programs provide intensive structure for people receiving treatment who are able to return to a safe home or other setting at the end of the day. Consumers typically arrive in the morning and participate in an extensive recovery program throughout the day, possibly extending into the evening. Common services include individual and group counseling, educational sessions, practice in recovery and relapse prevention skills, an introduction to GA, discharge planning, and family educational and counseling sessions.

Community mental health centers, family service agencies, community action programs, independent gambling treatment programs, psychiatric hospitals, general hospitals, and private counselors and psychotherapists all offer counseling services. Common services include individual and group counseling, educational sessions, practice in recovery and relapse prevention skills, an introduction to GA, discharge planning, and family educational and counseling sessions.

The most common 12-step group for gamblers is GA. GA is a voluntary fellowship of men and women who share their experiences with one another in an effort to stop compulsive gambling. Recovery is maintained through sharing experiences at group meetings and through the 12 steps for recovery from compulsive gambling.

Eligibility Criteria

Eligibility for services is based on each program's intake criteria. Such criteria may include evidence of compulsive gambling, treatment history, insurance coverage, and ability to pay. Funding sources include private health insurance, Medicaid, Medicare, military insurance, and self-payment. Membership in GA is available to all gambling addicts.

Contact Information

Contact government-sponsored state and local substance abuse agencies, public- and private-sector addictions programs, local health departments, community mental health agencies, family service agencies, community action programs, hospital social service departments, clergy, and the local contacts for GA.

Food

Services and Benefits

A variety of service providers offer treatment for food addiction and related eating disorders in a variety of settings. Residential treatment settings include independent rehabilitation programs, hospital inpatient programs, halfway houses, and 3/4-way houses. Community-based and outpatient program settings include partial hospitalization and day treatment programs, counseling, and 12-step meetings.

Independent rehabilitation program services typically include individual and group counseling; educational sessions; practice in recovery and relapse prevention skills; introduction to Overeaters Anonymous (OA), Food Addicts in Recovery Anonymous (FA), and other 12-step groups;

discharge planning; and family educational and counseling sessions. Residential services may be short term (30 days or less) or long term (more than 30 days).

Hospital inpatient services typically include individual and group counseling; educational sessions; practice in recovery and relapse prevention skills; introduction to OA, FA, and other 12-step groups; discharge planning; and family educational and counseling sessions. Residential services may be short term (30 days or less) or long term (more than 30 days).

A halfway house or 3/4-way house can provide a structured, community-based setting for people receiving treatment and counseling for food addiction and eating disorders. Halfway houses provide more structure and supervision than do 3/4-way houses. Typical services include individual and group counseling; educational sessions; practice in recovery and relapse prevention skills; introduction to OA, FA, and other 12-step groups; discharge planning; and family educational and counseling sessions Residential services may be short term (30 days or less) or long term (more than 30 days).

Partial hospitalization and day treatment programs provide intensive structure for people receiving treatment who are able to return to a safe home or other environment at the end of the day. Consumers typically arrive in the morning and participate in an extensive recovery program throughout the day, possibly extending into the evening. Common services include individual and group counseling; educational sessions; practice in recovery and relapse prevention skills; introduction to OA, FA, and other 12-step groups; discharge planning; and family educational and counseling sessions.

Community mental health centers, family service agencies, community action programs, independent food addiction treatment programs, eating disorders programs, psychiatric hospitals, general hospitals, and private counselors and psychotherapists all offer counseling services. Common services include individual and group counseling; educational sessions; practice in recovery and relapse prevention skills; introduction to OA, FA, and other 12-step groups; discharge planning; and family educational and counseling sessions.

The most common 12-step groups for food addicts are OA and FA. OA and FA are voluntary fellowships of men and women who share their experiences with one another in an effort to deal with food addiction. Recovery is maintained through sharing experiences at group meetings and through the 12 steps for recovery from food addiction.

ELIGIBILITY CRITERIA

Eligibility for services is based on each program's intake criteria. Such criteria may include evidence of food addiction, treatment history, insurance coverage, and ability to pay. Funding sources include private health insurance, Medicaid, Medicare, military insurance, and self-payment. Membership in OA, FA, and other 12-step groups is available to all food addicts.

CONTACT INFORMATION

Contact state and local government-sponsored addictions departments, public- and private-sector addictions programs, local health departments, community mental health agencies, family service agencies, community action programs, hospital social service departments, clergy, and the local contacts for OA, FA, and other 12-step groups.

Nicotine

SERVICES AND BENEFITS

A variety of service providers offer treatment for nicotine addiction in a variety of settings. Nicotine addiction programs generally use or combine elements from four major treatment approaches: nicotine replacement, non-nicotine therapy, behavioral treatment, and 12-step meetings.

Nicotine replacement treatment uses nicotine gum, the transdermal patch, nasal spray, or inhalers to relieve nicotine withdrawal symptoms. A prominent non-nicotine treatment therapy makes use of the prescription antidepressant drug bupropion. Behavioral treatment emphasizes various smoking cessation programs that help smokers discover high-risk relapse situations, create an aversion to smoking, develop self-monitoring of smoking behavior, and establish effective coping skills. Nicotine Anonymous is a voluntary fellowship of men and women who share their experiences with one another in an effort to deal with nicotine addiction. Recovery is maintained through sharing experiences at group meetings and through the 12 steps for recovery from nicotine addiction.

ELIGIBILITY CRITERIA

Eligibility for services is based on each program's specific intake criteria. Such criteria may include evidence of nicotine addiction, treatment history, insurance coverage, and ability to pay. Funding sources include private health insurance, Medicaid, Medicare, military insurance, and self-payment. Membership in Nicotine Anonymous is available to all nicotine addicts.

CONTACT INFORMATION

Contact state and local government-sponsored substance abuse departments, public- and private-sector addictions programs, departments of health, hospital social service departments, and the local contacts for Nicotine Anonymous.

Internet and Computer

SERVICES AND BENEFITS

Community-based counseling is available from a variety of sources, including clinical social workers, psychologists, psychiatrists, mental health counselors, and psychiatric nurses who have specialized training. Common treatment models include cognitive therapy, marriage and family therapy, and support groups. Counseling is available in person, by telephone, and online. Some treatment providers prescribe psychotropic medication.

ELIGIBILITY CRITERIA

Eligibility for services is based on each program's intake criteria. Such criteria may include evidence of computer and Internet addiction, treatment history, insurance coverage, and ability to pay. Funding sources include private health insurance, Medicaid, Medicare, military insurance, and self-payment.

CONTACT INFORMATION
Contact mental health professionals who specialize in the treatment of this phenomenon. Referrals may be obtained from clinical societies, professional associations, and directories of mental health professionals that list practitioners' specializations.

Sex

SERVICES AND BENEFITS
Community-based counseling is available from a variety of sources, including clinical social workers, psychologists, psychiatrists, mental health counselors, and psychiatric nurses who have specialized training. Residential treatment is available in facilities that also treat other types of addiction. Common treatment models involve the use of cognitive-behavioral therapy, self-help groups, and a 12-step program, Sex Addicts Anonymous. Some treatment providers prescribe psychotropic medication.

ELIGIBILITY CRITERIA
Eligibility for services is based on each program's intake criteria. Such criteria may include evidence of sex addiction, treatment history, insurance coverage, and ability to pay. Funding sources include private health insurance, Medicaid, Medicare, military insurance, and self-payment. Membership in Sex Addicts Anonymous and other related 12-step programs is available to all sex addicts.

CONTACT INFORMATION
Contact state and local government-sponsored addictions departments, departments of health, hospital social service departments, and the local contacts for Sex Addicts Anonymous.

Spending and Shopping

SERVICES AND BENEFITS

Community-based counseling is available from a variety of sources, including clinical social workers, psychologists, psychiatrists, mental health counselors, and psychiatric nurses who have specialized training. Residential treatment is available in facilities that also treat other types of addiction. Common treatment models involve the use of cognitive–behavioral therapy; self-help groups; and a 12-step program, Debtors Anonymous. Some treatment providers prescribe psychotropic medication.

ELIGIBILITY CRITERIA

Eligibility for services is based on each program's intake criteria. Such criteria may include evidence of spending and shopping addiction, treatment history, insurance coverage, and ability to pay. Funding sources include private health insurance, Medicaid, Medicare, military insurance, and self-payment. Membership in Debtors Anonymous and other related 12-step programs is available to all spending and shopping addicts.

CONTACT INFORMATION

Contact state and local government-sponsored addictions departments, health departments, hospital social service departments, and the local contacts for Debtors Anonymous.

Useful Tips

A variety of organizations make available information about addictions in general and specific addictions. Consult the informational Web sites of organizations such as

- Alcoholics Anonymous (http://www.aa.org/)
- the Center for Substance Abuse Treatment, Substance Abuse and Mental Health Services Administration (http://csat.samhsa.gov/)
- Cocaine Anonymous (http://www.ca.org/)
- Debtors Anonymous (http://www.debtorsanonymous.org/)

- Food Addicts in Recovery Anonymous (http://foodaddicts anonymous.org/)
- Gamblers Anonymous (http://www.gamblersanonymous.org/)
- Medication Assisted Therapies, the Center for Substance Abuse Treatment, Substance Abuse and Mental Health Services Administration (http://dpt.samhsa.gov/)
- Methadone Anonymous (http://www.methadonesupport.org/)
- Narcotics Anonymous, (http://www.na.org/)
- the National Clearinghouse for Alcohol and Drug Information, Substance Abuse and Mental Health Services Administration (http://ncadi.samhsa.gov/)
- the National Council on Problem Gambling (http://www.ncpgambling.org/)
- the National Institute on Drug Abuse, National Institutes of Health (http://www.drugabuse.gov/)
- Nicotine Anonymous (http://www.nicotine-anonymous.org/)
- Overeaters Anonymous (http://www.overeatersanonymous.org/)
- Quit Smoking Action Plan, the American Lung Association (http://www.lungusa.org/site/pp.asp?c=dvLUK9O0E&b=117062)
- Quitting Tips (tobacco use), the American Cancer Society (http://www.cancer.org/docroot/PED/ped_10_3.asp?sitearea=PED)
- Sex Addicts Anonymous (http://www.sexaa.org/)
- the Substance Abuse and Mental Health Services Administration, U.S. Department of Health and Human Services (HHA) (http://www.samhsa.gov)
- the Substance Abuse Treatment Facility Locator, Center for Substance Abuse Treatment, Substance Abuse and Mental Health Services Administration (http://findtreatment.samhsa.gov/)
- You Can Quit Smoking Now! from the National Cancer Institute, Centers for Disease Control and Prevention, and National Institutes of Health (http://www.smokefree.gov/) .

Sexual Orientation

Overview

SEXUAL ORIENTATION INVOLVES people's preference for sexual activity with members of their own sex (homosexual orientation), the opposite sex (heterosexual orientation), or both sexes (bisexual orientation). Sexual orientation is based on the nature of a person's attraction, behavior, and identity. A person may feel sexual attraction to people of the same or opposite sex, or to both. A person's sexual behavior may involve engaging in sexual activity with partners of the same or opposite sex. Sexual identity refers to a person's view of himself or herself as heterosexual, homosexual, bisexual, or transgender.

Many services are available to lesbians (women with a homosexual orientation), gay men (men with a homosexual orientation), bisexuals (people who are sexually attracted to males and females), people who are transgender (those who express their sexuality by fully or partially reversing gender roles, such as transvestites, transsexuals, and cross-dressers), or anyone who may seek assistance with sexual orientation issues. Important issues that may arise in relation to sexual orientation include mental health, schools and youths, parenting and families, civil rights, and hate crimes.

Mental Health

SERVICES AND BENEFITS

A wide variety of professionals and agencies provide mental health services related to lesbian, gay, bisexual, and transgender (LGBT) issues. Agencies

105

that specialize in offering counseling and mental health services related to LGBT issues may include community-based agencies that specialize in LGBT issues; community mental health centers; family service agencies; community action programs; hospital psychiatry and outpatient clinics; and independent clinical social workers, psychologists, psychiatrists, mental health counselors, psychiatric nurses, and pastoral counselors. Online services also are available.

ELIGIBILITY CRITERIA
Eligibility for mental health and counseling services depends on various criteria, such as mental health needs, clinical diagnosis, age, community of residence, and insurance coverage.

CONTACT INFORMATION
Contact agencies that focus on LGBT issues, community mental health centers, family service agencies, hospital psychiatry and outpatient clinics, private counselors, clergy, and other organizations and professionals familiar with local mental health resources.

Schools and Youths

SERVICES AND BENEFITS
Many programs and services can assist LGBT youths who struggle with sexual orientation issues or who face harassment or abuse, such as antigay slurs, insults, and homophobic remarks or physical assaults, in school settings. Local agencies and advocates can help youths meet with school administrators; organize and participate in gay and straight alliances, community groups for LGBT youths, safe school coalitions, and sensitivity training sessions for school staff and students; lobby school boards for nondiscrimination policies; advocate for legislation that protects LGBT youths; encourage diversification of school curricula; support families that have lost loved ones because of harassment or abuse of LGBT youths at school; work with parent–teacher associations and other groups; monitor schools' compliance with nondiscrimination policies; support LGBT faculty and staff; and disseminate information about LGBT issues.

ELIGIBILITY CRITERIA
Programs and agencies concerned with LGBT issues generally invite all interested parties to participate in their efforts.

CONTACT INFORMATION
Contact programs and agencies that focus on LGBT issues, such as local chapters of Parents, Families, and Friends of Lesbians and Gays (PFLAG) and agencies that serve LGBT youths.

Parenting and Families

SERVICES AND BENEFITS
In many communities, services and information related to LGBT parenting and families are available from agencies that specialize in LGBT issues, community mental health centers, family service agencies, community action programs, hospital psychiatry and outpatient clinics, independent clinical social workers, psychologists, psychiatrists, mental health counselors, psychiatric nurses, and pastoral counselors. Online services and information also are available.

ELIGIBILITY CRITERIA
Programs and agencies concerned with LGBT issues generally invite all parents and family members to participate in their efforts.

CONTACT INFORMATION
Contact programs and agencies that focus on LGBT issues, such as local chapters of PFLAG and agencies that serve LGBT youths.

Civil Rights and Hate Crimes

SERVICES AND BENEFITS
Several organizations offer information and assistance to people who are concerned about LGBT-related civil rights and hate crimes. Services are available related to

- aging, involving issues related to discrimination against older LGBT people and advance legal planning, such as estate planning, advance directives, durable powers of attorney, and living wills;
- civil unions, involving issues related to gay and lesbian relationships;
- criminal law, focusing on criminal statutes related to same-sex relations that affect prosecution, employment, child custody, and other life issues;
- discrimination, particularly in relation to laws that affect employment, public accommodations, housing, credit, union practices, education, and the military;
- domestic partnerships and domestic partner benefits;
- employment issues, in relation to workplace discrimination and protection issues, hiring and firing practices and policies, and benefits issues;
- family issues, particularly legal protections related to adoption, foster care, custody, guardianship, and inheritance;
- hate crimes and antigay violence, slurs, and homophobia;
- HIV/AIDS issues, in relation to bias in employment, access to housing and health care services, and rights to privacy;
- housing and public accommodations, promoting equal access to rental housing, homeownership, and other public accommodations;
- immigration and asylum, focusing on the asylum rights of people who reasonably fear prosecution in their home countries because of their sexual orientation;
- marriage issues related to gay and lesbian marriage;
- reproductive rights issues, such as those involving abortion and reproductive rights and options;
- school and youth issues, such as those involving discrimination in school policy and practice, and antigay violence.

ELIGIBILITY CRITERIA
Civil rights organizations generally make their services available to anyone who is a victim of civil rights violations and hate crimes.

Contact organizations concerned with civil rights in general, such as the American Civil Liberties Union, or organizations concerned with the rights of LGBT people, such as PFLAG, the Lambda Legal Defense and Education Fund, and the Gay and Lesbian Alliance Against Defamation.

Useful Tips

Additional information about sexual orientation issues and specific LGBT issues can be obtained from

- the American Civil Liberties Union (http://www.aclu.org/)
- Children of Lesbians and Gays Everywhere (COLAGE; http://www.colage.org/)
- the Family Pride Coalition (http://www.familypride.org)
- the Gay Asian Pacific Support Network (http://www.gapsn.org/)
- the Gay Student Center (http://gaystudentcenter.studentcenter.org/)
- the Gay, Lesbian, Straight Education Network (GLSEN; http://www.glsen.org)
- Gay and Lesbian Alliance Against Defamation (GLAAD; http://www.glaad.org/)
- the GLBT National Help Center (http://www.glnh.org/)
- Gay Men's Health Crisis (http://www.gmhc.org/)
- the Lambda Legal Defense and Education Fund (http://www.lambdalegal.org)
- the National Center for Lesbian Rights (http://www.nclrights.org/)
- the National Gay and Lesbian Task Force (http://www.thetaskforce.org/)
- OutProud, the National Coalition for Gay, Lesbian, Bisexual, and Transgender Youth (http://www.outproud.org/)
- Parents, Families and Friends of Lesbians and Gays (PFLAG; http://www.pflag.org/)

- the Trevor Project, national suicide prevention helpline for LGBTQ youths (http://www.thetrevorproject.org/)
- Trikone, serving lesbian, gay, bisexual, and transgender South Asians (http://www.trikone.org/)
- YouthResource, a Web site for gay, lesbian, bisexual, transgender, and questioning youths (http://www.youthresource.com/).

FAMILY LIFE EDUCATION

Overview

FAMILY LIFE EDUCATION includes a variety of programs and services designed to strengthen families. Many social service agencies sponsor programs that provide family members with important knowledge and skills.

SERVICES AND BENEFITS
Family life education programs address a broad range of topics and issues, such as

- adolescent development, identifying typical stages, developmental milestones, and challenges that occur during adolescence and offering practical strategies to help adults parent their adolescent children effectively;
- adoption, addressing common themes and challenges that emerge in adoptive families and fostering practical adoptive parenting skills;
- aging and elder care, identifying typical stages, developmental milestones, and challenges that occur throughout the aging process and offering practical strategies to help adults cope with and manage aging and elder care;
- child development, identifying typical stages, developmental milestones, and challenges that occur during childhood, as well as practical strategies to help adults parent their children effectively;

111

- communication and couples, addressing ways to enhance communication between spouses and partners;
- conflict resolution, offering practical strategies for addressing and resolving conflict among family members;
- disabilities, addressing common issues, themes, and challenges that emerge when coping with a disability or caring for a family member who has a disability and offering practical skills to help family members cope with disabilities;
- death and dying, addressing common issues, themes, and challenges that emerge during the dying process and following the death of a relative or loved one and offering practical skills to help family members cope with dying and death;
- family dynamics, addressing common issues, themes, and challenges that emerge in families;
- grief and loss, including common issues, themes, and challenges that emerge following major loss that occurs from death, miscarriage, divorce, and other significant events and offering practical skills to help family members cope with loss;
- mental illness, including how to recognize signs of mental illness and strategies for coping with mental illness;
- mental health, offering practical strategies to promote and enhance mental health;
- nutrition, addressing nutrition guidelines and practical strategies to enhance family members' nutrition;
- parenting and stepparenting skills, addressing common issues, themes, and challenges that emerge in parenting and stepparenting and offering practical parenting and stepparenting skills;
- posttraumatic stress, exploring the ways in which people respond to traumatic events in their lives and constructive responses to trauma victims;
- resettlement, offering practical knowledge and skills to enhance the resettlement of immigrants and refugees, which may include information about language, community resources, government services, education, finances, health care, and employment;

- self-esteem, addressing the nature of self-esteem and offering practical strategies to enhance self-esteem;
- separation and divorce, addressing common issues, themes, and challenges that emerge in families during separation and divorce and offering practical skills to help family members cope with separation and divorce;
- spirituality and the family, exploring the nature of spirituality and the role of spirituality in family life;
- stress management, addressing the nature, sources, and manifestations of stress in daily life and offering practical strategies for coping with stress;
- substance abuse, addressing the nature of substance abuse, warning signs, and offering practical strategies for coping with substance abuse among family members.

ELIGIBILITY CRITERIA
Sponsors of family life education typically accept anyone who is interested in the topics addressed in workshops.

CONTACT INFORMATION
Contact sponsors of family life education programs, such as family service agencies, community mental health centers, community action programs, and hospitals.

Useful Tips

Family services agencies; community mental health centers; community action programs; hospitals; and other continuing education programs, such as those given by colleges and universities, offer a great deal of information about family life education. Information sources and sponsors of family life education include

- the Alliance for Children and Families, an organization of family service agencies throughout the United States and Canada (http://www.alliance1.org/)

- the Community Action Partnership, an association of community action programs (http://www.communityactionpartnership.com)
- the National Mental Health Information Center, Substance Abuse and Mental Health Services Administration (http://mentalhealth. samhsa.gov/topics/)
- Services for Families, a site operated by the Administration on Children, Youth, and Families (http://www.acf.hhs.gov/acf_ services.html)
- USA.gov, online information about family issues from the U.S. Government (http://www.usa.gov/Citizen/Topics/Family_Issues. shtml).

CHILDREN AND
ADOLESCENTS

Overview

A WIDE RANGE of social services is available to assist children and adolescents. Some services, such as adoption and early intervention programs, are targeted for very young children. Other services—such as after-school mentoring, peer-mediation, and crisis intervention—focus on older children and adolescents.

Services for children and adolescents can be placed in several broad categories: child welfare services; crisis services; and educational, recreational, and enrichment services.

Child Welfare Services

Child welfare services are available to care for children and adolescents whose parents or birth parents are unable to care for them or who need supplemental care to enhance their development. Important child welfare services and programs include foster care, adoption, early intervention services, Head Start programs, independent living programs, and court-appointed advocates or guardians.

Foster Care

SERVICES AND BENEFITS
Foster care includes temporary care in family settings for children who are unable to live with their parents or guardians because of child abuse,

child neglect, insufficient resources, or parents' and guardians' difficulty managing children's behavior. Therapeutic foster care, a specialized form of foster care, includes services for children with significant emotional or behavioral problems.

ELIGIBILITY CRITERIA

Foster care programs are available for children in need of emergency and long-term placement. Eligibility may be based on evidence of child abuse, child neglect, parents' and guardians' resources, and parents' and guardians' difficulty managing children's behavior.

CONTACT INFORMATION

Contact state and county child welfare agencies that administer foster care programs or independent and private foster care agencies that have contracts with public child welfare agencies.

Adoption

SERVICES AND BENEFITS

Adoption occurs when courts create a special parent–child relationship between a child and adults who are not related by blood. Adoption is the legal act of terminating the parental responsibilities of the biological parents of a child and transferring those responsibilities to adoptive parents. The adopted child is entitled to all privileges ordinarily granted to a biological child. Various programs and options are available to facilitate domestic and international adoption, and for adoption of infants and older children, children of color, and children with disabilities, among others.

ELIGIBILITY CRITERIA

Prospective adoptive parents are screened by adoption agencies and professionals who are authorized to conduct comprehensive assessments and "home studies." Eligibility criteria vary among adoption agencies; some agencies have more stringent eligibility criteria than others with regard to marital status, income, health risks, and other factors.

CONTACT INFORMATION

Contact state and local child welfare agencies, independent adoption agencies and organizations, and independent adoption professionals and attorneys.

Early Intervention

SERVICES AND BENEFITS

Early intervention programs provide services to the families of infants and toddlers (birth to age three) with disabilities and who are at risk for developmental delays. Typical services include early identification, screening, and assessment services; assistive technology; audiology (hearing) services; family resource coordination; family training and counseling; health services; nursing services; nutrition services; occupational therapy; physical therapy; psychological and social work services; speech and language services; transportation services; and vision services. Services may be provided in the child's home, child care centers, family day care homes, recreational centers, playgrounds, play groups, libraries, and other settings where children and parents go for fun and support.

ELIGIBILITY CRITERIA

Eligibility for early intervention services is based on the nature and extent of a child's delay in one or more developmental areas, such as a cognitive, physical, emotional, social, or communication delay.

CONTACT INFORMATION

Contact the state or local agency or agencies responsible for administering the early intervention program. Such agencies might include the state or county department of health, department of social services, department of disabilities, or department of rehabilitation.

Head Start and Early Head Start

SERVICES AND BENEFITS

Head Start and Early Head Start are comprehensive child development programs that serve children from birth to age five, as well as pregnant women and their families. The primary goal of Early Head Start is enhancement of prenatal outcomes, healthy development of infants and toddlers, and healthy family functioning. The primary goal of Head Start is enhancement of the school readiness of young children in low-income families. Typical services include education about early childhood development, preschool education, medical care, dental care, and nutrition counseling.

ELIGIBILITY CRITERIA
Eligibility for Head Start and Early Head Start is based on applicant's (child's) age, and family income.

CONTACT INFORMATION
Contact local agencies that administer the Head Start and Early Head Start programs, such as family service agencies, community action programs, public child welfare agencies, and independent Head Start programs.

Independent Living

SERVICES AND BENEFITS
Independent living programs are designed to help adolescents and young adults develop the skills they need to live independently. Many programs serve people who do not have stable families and are living in foster care. Typical services include practice in daily living skills, case management, money management, career and educational planning, mental health services, housing assistance, and recreational and social activities.

ELIGIBILITY CRITERIA
Eligibility for independent living programs varies based on criteria such as age, family circumstances and special needs, program funding sources, and populations served.

CONTACT INFORMATION
Contact state and local child welfare agencies, foster care programs, family service agencies, and departments of human services.

Court-Appointed Special Advocates or Guardians ad Litem

SERVICES AND BENEFITS

Court-appointed special advocates (CASA) programs and guardian ad litem (GAL) programs assign trained volunteers who advocate on behalf of children in court. CASA and GAL programs assist youths who have been abused, neglected, or charged as wayward children or delinquents. Typical services include conducting an independent investigation of the child and the child's circumstances, reporting information to the judge through written reports and court testimony, advocating in court for the child's best interests, and monitoring compliance with court orders.

ELIGIBILITY CRITERIA

Participation in CASA or GAL programs is based on juvenile or family court policies and procedures.

CONTACT INFORMATION

Contact the local CASA office or local juvenile or family court.

Crisis Services

Many children and adolescents find themselves in crisis circumstances. Some children and youths run away from home or are kidnapped; abuse drugs and alcohol; skip school; or engage in dangerous, out-of-control behaviors. Important crisis services and programs include missing children programs, substance abuse and drug court programs, programs to address truancy, and therapeutic schools and programs.

Missing Children

SERVICES AND BENEFITS

Several national and local agencies help to locate missing children. Missing children may have run away from home, may have been abducted by a stranger or family member, or may be victims of sexual exploitation.

Typical services for missing children and their families include investigation, advocacy, and distribution of information about missing children.

Eligibility Criteria
Agencies provide services when there is evidence that a child is missing.

Contact Information
Contact public and private organizations that help locate missing children, including law enforcement and public child welfare agencies.

Substance Abuse and Drug Court

Services and Benefits
A wide range of services is available to youths who are abusing drugs or alcohol. Youths who need these services sometimes fall under the jurisdiction of a substance abuse court or drug court. A *drug court* is a special court given the responsibility to handle substance-abusing youths through comprehensive supervision, drug testing, treatment services, sanctions, and incentives such as avoiding jail and prison. Plans for offenders are developed by judges, prosecutors, defense counsel, substance abuse treatment professionals, probation officers, law enforcement and corrections officials, educational and vocational personnel, community leaders, and others.

Drug courts refer youths to many different residential and outpatient services. Residential services include detoxification programs, independent rehabilitation programs, hospital inpatient programs, halfway houses, and 3/4-way houses. Community-based and outpatient programs include partial hospitalization and day treatment programs, counseling, and 12-step meetings.

Detoxification programs provide medically monitored care of youths who are having acute problems resulting from withdrawal from alcohol or drug use. Typical services include physical examination; nursing evaluation; biopsychosocial assessment; monitoring for withdrawal complications, such as elevated vital signs, tremors, sweats, or seizures; medical treatment and hospital care; special diets; individual and group counseling; family involvement; and discharge planning.

Independent rehabilitation programs typically offer individual and group counseling; educational sessions; practice in recovery and relapse prevention skills; introduction to 12-step programs, such as AA, NA, CA, or MA; discharge planning; and family educational and counseling sessions. Programs may be short term (30 days or less) or long term (more than 30 days).

Hospital inpatient programs offer services that typically include individual and group counseling, educational sessions, practice in recovery and relapse prevention skills, introduction to 12-step programs, discharge planning, and family educational and counseling sessions. Residential services may be short term (30 days or less) or long term (more than 30 days).

A halfway house or 3/4-way house provides a structured, community-based setting for youths receiving treatment and counseling for alcoholism or drug abuse. Halfway houses provide more structure and supervision than do 3/4-way houses. Typical services include individual and group counseling, educational sessions, practice in recovery and relapse prevention skills, introduction to 12-step programs, discharge planning, and family educational and counseling sessions. Programs may be short term (30 days or less) or long term (more than 30 days).

Partial hospitalization and day treatment programs provide intensive structure for youths receiving treatment who are able to return to a safe home or other setting at the end of the day. Program participants typically arrive in the morning and take part in an extensive recovery program throughout the day, possibly continuing into the evening. Common services include individual and group counseling, educational sessions, practice in recovery and relapse prevention skills, introduction to 12-step programs, discharge planning, and family educational and counseling sessions.

Counseling services are available from community mental health centers, family service agencies, community action programs, independent alcoholism or drug treatment programs, psychiatric hospitals, general hospitals, and private counselors and psychotherapists. Common services include individual and group counseling, educational sessions, practice in recovery and relapse prevention skills, introduction to 12-step programs, discharge planning, and family educational and counseling sessions.

The most common 12-step groups for youths are AA, NA, CA, and MA. These are voluntary fellowships of youths who share their experiences with one another in an effort to attain and maintain sobriety and abstain from drug use. They are programs of total abstinence. Sobriety and abstinence are maintained through sharing experiences at group meetings and through the 12 steps for recovery from alcoholism.

ELIGIBILITY CRITERIA

Eligibility for services is based on each program's intake criteria. Such criteria may include evidence of alcoholism or substance abuse, treatment history, age, insurance coverage, and ability to pay. Funding sources include private health insurance, Medicaid, Medicare, and self-payment by the adolescent or the family. The only requirement for membership in 12-step programs is a desire to stop drinking and abusing drugs.

CONTACT INFORMATION

Information about alcohol treatment programs and drug courts is available from state and local substance abuse departments (for example, the state division of substance abuse), health departments, community mental health agencies, substance abuse treatment programs, family service agencies, community action programs, hospital social service departments, clergy, public defenders' offices, court personnel, and the local contacts for 12-step programs.

Truancy and Truancy Court

SERVICES AND BENEFITS

School districts and departments offer a variety of services to prevent or respond to truancy and school dropout. Typical services include intensive supervision of youths, supportive services, mental health services, and supportive services to parents.

Many communities sponsor truancy courts. Truancy courts are designed to enhance school attendance by using a supportive and nurturing approach rather than a punitive one. Truancy court judges, social workers and other mental health professionals, and school personnel design comprehensive treatment and prevention programs and services.

Typical services include case management, counseling, tutoring, and parent education.

ELIGIBILITY CRITERIA
Eligibility criteria for participation in truancy and truancy court programs vary among school districts and departments. Typical criteria include students' age, attendance record, behavior history, and academic standing.

CONTACT INFORMATION
Contact local school districts and departments, state and county departments of education, and local juvenile and family courts.

Therapeutic Schools and Programs

SERVICES AND BENEFITS
A variety of therapeutic schools serve youths who struggle with significant behavioral, mental health, and substance abuse issues. They range from locked and secure treatment centers to wilderness therapy programs. Prominent models include

- residential treatment centers, which offer highly structured and comprehensive treatment programs that provide mental health, therapeutic, educational, family, and other services to children and adolescents with significant mental health, behavioral, and substance abuse issues;
- day treatment and partial hospitalization programs, which provide youths with comprehensive nonresidential therapeutic services to help them address mental health, behavioral, and substance abuse issues;
- therapeutic boarding schools, which offer highly structured programs featuring mental health and therapeutic services along with a comprehensive educational program;
- emotional growth boarding schools, which offer structured programs that focus on residents' emotional development and personal growth but do not provide the intensive treatment services offered by therapeutic boarding schools;

- wilderness therapy programs, which have their roots in outdoor survival programs, offer highly structured therapeutic programs in remote locations that give adolescents an opportunity to address personal struggles without the distractions of their home environment and, through individual and group counseling, esteem-building experiences, and instruction in survival skills, develop self-confidence, teamwork skills, and self-esteem;
- alternative high schools, which provide education to adolescents who have foundered academically or socially in traditional high schools.

Eligibility Criteria
Eligibility criteria vary among programs. Such criteria typically include applicants' mental health needs and history, behavior history and challenges, academic history and standing, disabilities, age, gender, and ability to pay.

Contact Information
Contact independent educational consultants, directories and listings of programs for struggling youths, school guidance counselors and social service personnel, student assistance personnel, and social service staff in psychiatric and mental health programs that serve youths.

Educational, Recreational, and Enrichment Services

Many services and programs are available to enhance the development of children and youths. These programs range from after-school enrichment programs and summer camp experiences to programs designed to prevent pregnancy and bullying. Important services and programs include mentoring programs, after-school programs, camp programs, sex education, and bullying prevention programs.

Mentoring

Services and Benefits
Mentoring programs establish one-to-one relationships between adults and youths in an effort to prevent delinquency, school dropout, substance abuse, gang activity, and other high-risk behaviors. Mentoring programs are designed to provide guidance and support to youths, promote

personal and social responsibility, enhance students' educational experiences, discourage use of drugs and alcohol, prevent violence and gang activity, and encourage participation in community activities.

ELIGIBILITY CRITERIA
Eligibility criteria vary among programs. Such criteria typically include age; gender; community of residence; academic standing; family circumstances; and special needs, such as emotional and behavioral issues or disabilities.

CONTACT INFORMATION
Contact local family service agencies, child welfare agencies, school guidance counselors and social workers, and student assistance personnel.

After-School Programs

SERVICES AND BENEFITS
After-school programs provide structured and supervised social and recreational opportunities to enhance youths' development and prevent delinquency, school dropout, substance abuse, gang activity, and other high-risk behaviors. Typical programs include sports, recreation, field trips, arts and crafts, and educational opportunities.

ELIGIBILITY CRITERIA
Eligibility criteria vary among programs. Such criteria typically include age, community of residence, and household income.

CONTACT INFORMATION
Contact local school districts, school guidance counselors and social workers, student assistance programs, family service agencies, and child welfare agencies.

Camp Programs

SERVICES AND BENEFITS
Diverse camps are available for youths in general and youths with special needs. Camping opportunities are available for summer, winter, and

spring vacation periods. In addition to general camps, specialty camps are available in many communities. Specialty camps focus on sports; wilderness and nature; community service; academics; language study; music; art; travel; weight loss; horseback riding; sailing; aviation; computing; dance; drama; farming; religious study; and special needs, such as behavior challenges, learning disabilities, and developmental delays.

ELIGIBILITY CRITERIA
Eligibility criteria vary among camps. Such criteria typically include age, gender, and special needs.

CONTACT INFORMATION
Contact local family service agencies, child welfare agencies, community centers, and national camping associations and directories.

Sex Education

SERVICES AND BENEFITS
Sex education programs provide comprehensive information to youths about such topics as sexually transmitted infections, reproduction, contraception, abstinence, pregnancy, adoption options, reproductive rights, sexual orientation, women's health, and men's health.

ELIGIBILITY CRITERIA
Eligibility criteria vary among sex education programs. Such criteria typically include age, segregation by gender, and parental or guardian permission.

CONTACT INFORMATION
Contact family service agencies, child welfare organizations, school guidance counselors and social workers, student assistance programs, pediatricians, public health programs, departments of health, and sex educators.

Bullying Prevention Programs

SERVICES AND BENEFITS
Various programs are available to prevent, respond to, and provide education about child and adolescent bullying. Common bullying behaviors

include teasing, calling names, pushing, pulling, hitting or attacking, spreading rumors, harassing, ignoring and ostracizing, and forcing another person to hand over money or possessions. Typical programs teach children and adolescents how to recognize bullying; understand what motivates the bully; and use practical skills to avoid, defuse, or deflect bullying behavior.

ELIGIBILITY CRITERIA
Bullying prevention programs are made available to children and adolescents in schools, after-school programs, camps, recreational programs, residential treatment programs, and juvenile correctional facilities.

CONTACT INFORMATION
Contact school guidance counselors and social workers, student assistance programs, personnel in after-school programs, mediation programs, family service agencies, community mental health centers, community action programs, camps, recreational programs, residential treatment programs, and juvenile correctional facilities.

Peer Mediation and Dispute Resolution

SERVICES AND BENEFITS
Peer mediation and dispute resolution programs are designed to help youths resolve conflict constructively. Peer mediation is a negotiation-based process for resolving disputes and conflicts in which a neutral third party acts as a moderator. Peer mediators are trained to assess the nature of the conflict, listen to the concerns of the participants, help participants generate possible alternatives, and help participants agree on acceptable solutions. Peer mediation and dispute resolution may be used with individual youths, groups of youths, or gangs.

ELIGIBILITY CRITERIA
Eligibility criteria vary from program to program. Such criteria typically include age, gender, permission from parent or guardian, and the nature of the conflict or dispute.

Contact school guidance counselors and social workers, student assistance programs, personnel in after-school programs, mediation programs, camps, recreational programs, residential treatment programs, and juvenile correctional facilities.

Useful Tips

Information about foster care is available from

- the Administration on Children, Youth, and Families, U.S. Department of Health and Human Services (http://faq.acf.hhs.gov/)
- American Foster Care Resources, Inc. (http://www.afcr.com/)
- Casey Family Services (http://www.caseyfamilyservices.org/)
- the Child Welfare League of America (http://www.cwla.org/programs/fostercare/)
- Foster Care Children (http://www.fostercarechildren.com/)
- the National Foster Parent Association (http://www.nfpainc.org).

Information about adoption is available from

- the Administration on Children, Youth, and Families (http://faq.acf.hhs.gov/)
- Adoption.com (http://www.adoption.com/)
- the Adoption Exchange Association (http://www.adoptea.org/)
- Adoption.org (http://www.adoption.org/)
- AdoptUSKids (http://www.adoptuskids.org/)
- the American Adoption Congress (http://www.americanadoptioncongress.org/)
- the Evan B. Donaldson Adoption Institute (http://www.adoptioninstitute.org/)
- Child Welfare Information Gateway (http://www.childwelfare.gov/adoption/)
- the Child Welfare League of America (http://www.cwla.org/programs/adoption/)
- the Dave Thomas Foundation for Adoption (http://www.davethomasfoundationforadoption.org/)

- the National Adoption Center (http://www.adopt.org/)
- the National Youth Violence Prevention Resource Center (http://www.safeyouth.org/scripts/topics/adoption.asp).

Information about early intervention is available from

- the Early Childhood Learning and Knowledge Center, Administration for Children and Families (http://eclkc.ohs.acf.hhs.gov/hslc)
- the Global Early Intervention Network (http://www.atsweb.neu.edu/cp/ei/)
- the International Society on Early Intervention (http://depts.washington.edu/isei/)
- Zero to Three (http://www.zerotothree.org/)

Information about Head Start and Early Head Start programs is available from

- the Early Childhood Learning and Knowledge Center, Administration for Children and Families (http://eclkc.ohs.acf.hhs.gov/hslc)
- the Office of Head Start, Administration for Children and Families (http://www.acf.hhs.gov/programs/ohs/)
- the National Head Start Association (http://www.nhsa.org/).

Information about independent living programs is available from

- Casey Family Services (http://www.caseyfamilyservices.org/)
- the Child Welfare League of America (http://www.cwla.org/programs/adoption/)
- the National Independent Living Association (http://www.nilausa.org/).

Information about court-appointed special advocates and guardians ad litem programs is available from

- CASAnet (http://www.casanet.org/)
- National CASA (http://www.nationalcasa.org/).

Information about missing children is available from

- KlaasKids National Search Center for Missing Children (http://www.klaaskids.org/search_center.htm)
- the National Center for Missing and Exploited Children (http://www.missingkids.com)
- the National Runaway Switchboard (http://www.1800runaway.org/)
- the National Youth Violence Prevention Resource Center (http://www.safeyouth.org/scripts/topics/missing.asp) and (http://www.safeyouth.org/scripts/topics/runaways.asp)
- USA.gov, official information from the U.S. Government (http://www.usa.gov/Citizen/Topics/Missing_Children.shtml)
- the Vanished Children's Alliance (http://www.vca.org/index.html)

Information about substance abuse and drug courts is available from

- Alcoholics Anonymous (http://www.aa.org/)
- the Center for Substance Abuse Treatment, Substance Abuse and Mental Health Services Administration (http://csat.samhsa.gov/)
- Cocaine Anonymous (http://www.ca.org/)
- the Drug Court Clearinghouse, Bureau of Justice Assistance (http://www1.spa.american.edu/justice/project.php?ID=1)
- Medication Assisted Therapies, the Center for Substance Abuse Treatment, Substance Abuse and Mental Health Services Administration (http://dpt.samhsa.gov/)
- Narcotics Anonymous (http://www.na.org/)
- the National Association of Drug Court Professionals (http://www.nadcp.org/)
- the National Youth Violence Prevention Resource Center, Centers for Disease Control and Prevention (http://www.safeyouth.org/scripts/topics/aabuse.asp) and (http://www.safeyouth.org/scripts/topics/subabuse.asp)
- the National Clearinghouse for Alcohol and Drug Information, Substance Abuse and Mental Health Services Administration (http://ncadi.samhsa.gov/)

- the National Institute on Drug Abuse, National Institutes of Health (http://www.drugabuse.gov/)
- the Substance Abuse and Mental Health Services Administration (http://www.samhsa.gov)
- the Substance Abuse Treatment Facility Locator, Center for Substance Abuse Treatment, Substance Abuse and Mental Health Services Administration (http://findtreatment.samhsa.gov/).

Information about truancy and truancy courts is available from

- the National Council of Juvenile and Family Court Judges (http://www.ncjfcj.org/)
- the National Youth Court Center (http://www.youthcourt.net/)
- the National Youth Violence Prevention Resource Center (http://www.safeyouth.org/scripts/topics/truancy.asp).

Information about therapeutic programs and schools is available from

- the Association of Boarding Schools (http://www.schools.com/)
- the Independent Educational Consultants Association (http://iecaonline.com/)
- the National Association of Therapeutic Schools and Programs (http://www.natsap.org/)
- Woodbury Reports (http://www.strugglingteens.com/).

Information about mentoring programs is available from

- America's Promise—The Alliance for Youth (http://www.americaspromise.org/)
- Big Brothers and Big Sisters of America (http://www.bbbsa.org)
- Boys and Girls Clubs of America (http://www.bgca.org/)
- Boy Scouts of America (http://www.scouting.org/)
- Camp Fire U.S.A. (http://www.campfireusa.org/)
- Communities in Schools (http://www.cisnet.org/)
- Friends of the Children (http://www.friendsofthechildren.org/)
- Girl Scouts of America (http://www.girlscouts.org/)
- Junior Achievement (http://www.ja.org/)

- Mentor: National Mentoring Partnership (http://www.mentoring. org/)
- the National Mentoring Center (http://www.nwrel.org/ mentoring/)
- National Youth Violence Prevention Resource Center (http:// www.safeyouth.org/scripts/topics/mentoring.asp)
- 100 Black Men of America (http://www.100blackmen.org/)
- the Tutor/Mentor Connection (http://www.tutormentor connection.org/)
- YouthFriends (http://www.youthfriends.org/)
- Youth Mentoring Connection (http://www.youthmentoring.org/).

Information about after-school programs is available from

- Afterschool.gov (http://www.afterschool.gov)
- Afterschool Alliance (http://www.afterschoolalliance.org)
- Aspiring Youth (http://www.aspiringyouth.org/)
- Big Brothers and Big Sisters of America (http://www.bbbsa.org)
- Boys and Girls Clubs of America (http://www.bgca.org/)
- Boy Scouts of America (http://www.scouting.org/)
- Camp Fire U.S.A. (http://www.campfireusa.org/)
- Communities in Schools (http://www.cisnet.org/)
- Girl Scouts of America (http://www.girlscouts.org/)
- Jewish Community Centers of North America (http://www.jcca. org/)
- the National After School Association (http://naaweb.your membership.com/)
- the National Youth Violence Prevention Resource Center (http:// www.safeyouth.org/scripts/topics/asprograms.asp)
- Promising Practices in Afterschool (http://www.afterschool.org/)
- YMCA (http://www.ymca.org)
- YWCA (http://www.ywca.org).

Information about camps and camping opportunities is available from

- the American Camping Association (http://www.acacamps.org/)
- the National Camp Association (http://www.summercamp.org/).

Information about sex education is available from

- Advocates for Youth (http://www.advocatesforyouth.org/)
- the American Association of Sex Educators, Counselors, and Therapists (http://www.aasect.org)
- the American Social Health Association (http://www.iwanna know.org/)
- the Coalition for Positive Sexuality (http://www.positive.org/)
- Go Ask Alice! (http://www.goaskalice.columbia.edu/)
- OutProud (http://www.outproud.org/)
- the Planned Parenthood Federation of America (http://www. teenwire.com/)
- the Resource Center for Adolescent Pregnancy Prevention (http://www.etr.org/recapp/)
- Sex, etc. (http://www.sxetc.org/).

Information about bullying is available from

- the Anti-bullying Network (http://www.antibullying.net/)
- bullying.org (http://www.bullying.org/)
- National Youth Violence Prevention Resource Center (http://www.safeyouth.org/scripts/topics/bullying.asp).

Information about peer mediation and dispute resolution programs is available from

- the Association for Conflict Resolution (http://www.acrnet.org/)
- the Center for Restorative Justice and Peacemaking (http://cehd. umn.edu/ssw/rjp/GEHS-3 housing.docx)
- the Conflict Resolution Information Source (http://www.crinfo.org/)
- the National Association for Community Mediation (http://www. nafcm.org/)
- Office of Dispute Resolution, U.S. Department of Justice (http:// www.usdoj.gov/odr/)
- Restorative Justice Online (http://www.restorativejustice.org/).

ABUSE AND NEGLECT: PROTECTIVE SERVICES

Overview

ADULTS AND CHILDREN sometimes are unable to take care of themselves, neglected by their caretakers, or victims of violence. For example, people with physical disabilities may not be properly cared for by family members, infants may be physically abused, elders may be neglected or exploited by their caretakers, and women may be victims of domestic violence or sexual assault.

Protective services programs provide assistance to victims of abuse and neglect. Programs typically specialize in services for children and youths, people with disabilities, women, and elderly people.

Children and Youths

SERVICES AND BENEFITS

Programs and services are available for children and youths who are unable to care for themselves; are neglected by their caretakers; or are victims of violence, such as sexual assault or domestic violence. Abuse and neglect can occur in various forms.

Physical abuse includes any physical injury inflicted other than by accidental means or inflicted as a result of mistreatment. Physical abuse also includes cruel punishment by someone responsible for the child's care. Examples of physical abuse include punching, kicking, biting, burning, twisting, beating, and hair pulling that causes head injuries. Physical abuse may cause internal injuries, cuts, bruises, lacerations, burns, scalds, or death.

Sexual abuse is sexual activity with children and adolescents that they do not fully comprehend, to which they are unable to give informed consent, or that violates current taboos and social standards. Sexual abuse involves any incident of sexual contact involving a child that is inflicted, or allowed to be inflicted, by someone responsible for the child's care. Examples of sexual abuse include rape; intercourse; sodomy; fondling; oral sex; incest; sexual penetration; and permitting, coercing, or forcing a child to participate in pornography or prostitution.

Emotional abuse is a pattern of behavior that attacks a child's emotional development and sense of self-worth. Examples of emotional abuse include repeated negative acts or statements to the child; exposure to repeated violent, brutal, or intimidating acts or statements among members of the child's household; cruel or unusual actions used in an attempt to gain submission, to enforce control, or to control the child's behavior; belittling; and rejection of the child.

Neglect is the intentional or unintentional failure of a person responsible for the child's care to provide and maintain adequate food, clothing, medical care, supervision, or education. Examples of neglect include abandoning a child, denying proper medical care and attention, and permitting a child to live under harsh conditions. Neglect can be physical, medical, educational, or mental and moral.

Examples of physical neglect include failing to provide adequate food, clothing, and shelter based on climatic conditions; failing to provide adequate child care; leaving a young child alone for an excessive period of time; holding the child responsible for the care of siblings or others beyond the child's ability. Physical neglect also occurs when the person responsible for the child's care is impaired or displays unstable behavior and when the person responsible for the child's care is unable to perform minimal child care tasks consistently. Examples of medical neglect include refusal or failure on the part of the person responsible for the child's care to seek, obtain, or maintain those services necessary for the child's medical, dental, and mental health needs, or withholding medically indicated treatment from children with serious medical conditions.

Examples of educational neglect include failing to enroll a child in school or failing to encourage or monitor the child's school attendance. Examples of emotional and moral neglect include encouraging the child to steal or sell drugs; encouraging the child to use drugs or alcohol; failing to address the child's emotional needs; and having inappropriate expectations of the child, considering the child's developmental level.

Services available to assist children and youths in need include crisis intervention, individual and family counseling, and parent education. Many agencies also provide services to family members and caretakers.

ELIGIBILITY CRITERIA

Eligibility criteria vary from program to program. Such criteria typically include evidence of abuse and neglect, social service needs, court orders, and ability to pay.

CONTACT INFORMATION

Contact state and local child protective service agencies; child welfare agencies; family service agencies; community mental health centers; community action programs; school guidance counselors and social workers; student assistance personnel; clergy; and independent counselors who provide services to children, youths, and their families.

People with Disabilities

SERVICES AND BENEFITS

Programs and services are available to assist people with disabilities who are unable to care for themselves; are neglected by their caretakers; or are victims of violence, such as sexual assault or domestic violence. Abuse can occur in many forms, including physical abuse, sexual abuse, emotional abuse, and financial abuse.

Physical abuse is any physical injury inflicted other than by accidental means or inflicted as a result of mistreatment. Physical abuse also can be cruel punishment by someone responsible for the person's care. Examples of physical abuse include punching, kicking, biting, burning, twisting, beating, or hair pulling that causes head injuries. Physical abuse may cause internal injuries, cuts, bruises, lacerations, burns, scalds, or death.

Sexual abuse is the involving of people with disabilities in any sexual activity that they do not fully comprehend, to which they are unable to give informed consent, or that violates current taboos and social standards. Sexual abuse involves any incident of sexual contact with a person with disabilities that is inflicted, or allowed to be inflicted, by someone responsible for that person's care. Examples of sexual abuse include rape; intercourse; sodomy; fondling; oral sex; incest; sexual penetration; and permitting, coercing, or forcing a person with disabilities to participate in pornography or prostitution.

Emotional abuse involves a pattern of behavior that attacks the emotional development and sense of self-worth of a person with disabilities. Examples of emotional abuse include repeated negative acts or statements to the person; exposure to repeated violent, brutal, or intimidating acts or statements among members of the person's household; cruel or unusual actions used in the attempt to gain submission or to control the person's behavior; belittling; and rejection of the person.

Financial abuse is any act involving the misuse or misappropriation of the money or property of a person with disabilities without that person's full knowledge and informed consent. Examples of financial abuse include theft of money and checks, misappropriation of funds, and misuse of a power of attorney.

Neglect involves the intentional or unintentional failure of a person responsible for the care of a person with disabilities to provide and maintain adequate food, clothing, medical care, supervision, or education. Examples of neglect include abandonment of a person with disabilities, denial of proper care and attention, and permitting a person with disabilities to live under harsh conditions. Neglect can be physical, medical, or emotional and moral. In some cases, a person with disabilities can neglect himself or herself.

Examples of physical neglect include failing to provide adequate food, clothing, and shelter based on climatic conditions; failing to provide adequate care; leaving a person with disabilities alone for an excessive period of time; or holding the person with disabilities responsible for the care of others beyond the person's ability. Neglect also occurs when the person responsible for the care of a person with disabilities is impaired or displays unstable behavior and when the person responsible for the care of a person with disabilities is unable to perform minimal care tasks consistently. Examples of medical neglect include refusing or failing to seek, obtain, or maintain those services necessary for the medical, dental, and mental health needs of the person with disabilities; or withholding medically indicated treatment from people with disabilities.

Examples of emotional and moral neglect include failing to address the emotional needs of a person with disabilities and having inappropriate expectations of the person considering his or her developmental level. Self-neglect also can occur. Examples of self-neglect include the failure of a person with disabilities to eat or to address his or her serious medical needs.

Services available to assist people with disabilities typically include crisis intervention, individual and family counseling, and family and caretaker education.

ELIGIBILITY CRITERIA
Eligibility criteria vary from program to program. Such criteria typically include evidence of abuse and neglect, social service needs, court orders, and ability to pay.

CONTACT INFORMATION
Contact state and local adult protective service agencies, and public and private agencies that provide state and local services to people with disabilities.

Women

SERVICES AND BENEFITS
Many programs and services are available for women who are victims of violence, such as sexual assault or domestic violence. Prominent examples of domestic violence and abuse against women include physical, sexual, and emotional abuse and sexual assault.

Physical abuse is any physical injury inflicted other than by accidental means or as a result of mistreatment or cruel punishment by someone against a woman. Examples of physical abuse include punching, kicking, biting, burning, twisting, beating, or hair pulling that causes head injuries. Physical abuse may cause internal injuries, cuts, bruises, lacerations, burns, scalds, or death.

Sexual abuse involves any incident of sexual contact that is inflicted, or allowed to be inflicted, by someone without the woman's fully informed consent. Examples of sexual abuse include rape; intercourse; sodomy; fondling; oral sex; incest; sexual penetration; and permitting, coercing, or forcing a woman to participate in pornography or prostitution.

Emotional abuse is a pattern of behavior that attacks the emotional development and sense of self-worth of a woman. Examples of emotional abuse include repeated negative acts or statements to the woman, cruel or unusual actions used in the attempt to gain submission or to control the woman's behavior, belittling and rejection of the woman, name calling or putdowns, withholding money, preventing a partner from contacting family or friends, stalking, and intimidation.

In addition to social services such as counseling and emergency housing, domestic violence programs also offer victims information and assistance related to restraining orders; no-contact orders; and orders of protection, which are court orders that prohibit a person from contacting or approaching another person.

ELIGIBILITY CRITERIA

Eligibility criteria vary from program to program. Such criteria typically include evidence of abuse and neglect, social service needs, court orders, and ability to pay.

CONTACT INFORMATION

Contact agencies that serve women, such as domestic violence programs, coalitions, and shelters; rape crisis and sexual assault centers; and women's centers. (Information about domestic violence perpetrated against men also is available from domestic violence programs, coalitions, and shelters.)

Elderly People

SERVICES AND BENEFITS

Programs and services are available to assist elders who are unable to care for themselves; are neglected by their caretakers; or are victims of violence, such as sexual assault or domestic violence. Abuse and neglect can occur in many forms, including physical, sexual, emotional, or financial abuse. Abuse and neglect of elderly people also may occur in institutional settings, such as nursing homes.

Physical abuse is any physical injury deliberately inflicted as a result of maltreatment or as cruel punishment by someone responsible for the care of an elderly person. Examples of physical abuse include punching, kicking, biting, burning, twisting, beating, or hair pulling that causes head injuries. Physical abuse may cause internal injuries, cuts, bruises, lacerations, burns, scalds, or death.

Sexual abuse is any sexual activity that the elderly person does not fully comprehend or to which he 'or she is unable to give informed consent. Sexual abuse involves any incident of sexual contact involving an elderly person that is inflicted, or allowed to be inflicted, by someone responsible for that person's care. Examples of sexual abuse include rape; intercourse; sodomy; fondling; oral sex; incest; sexual penetration; and permitting, coercing, or forcing an elderly person to participate in pornography or prostitution.

Emotional abuse involves a pattern of behavior that attacks the emotional development and sense of an elderly person. Examples of emotional abuse include repeated negative acts or statements to the elderly person; exposure to repeated violent, brutal, or intimidating acts or statements among members of the elderly person's household; cruel or unusual actions used in the attempt to gain submission or to control the elderly person's behavior; and belittling and rejection of the elderly person.

Financial abuse is any act involving the misuse or misappropriation of the money or property of an elderly person without that person's full knowledge and informed consent. Examples of financial abuse include theft of money and checks, misappropriation of funds, and misuse of a power of attorney.

Nursing home abuse is the harmful treatment of nursing home residents, which may range from rough handling to verbal abuse. Examples of nursing home abuse include physical abuse, sexual abuse, corporal punishment, verbal harassment, and involuntary seclusion.

Neglect is the intentional or unintentional failure of a person responsible for the care of an elderly person to provide and maintain adequate food, clothing, medical care, supervision, or education. Examples of neglect include abandoning an elderly person, denying the person proper care and attention, or permitting him or her to live under harsh conditions. Neglect can be physical, medical, or emotional and moral.

Examples of physical neglect include failing to provide adequate food, clothing, and shelter based on climatic conditions; failing to provide adequate care; leaving an elderly person alone for an excessive period of time; and holding the elderly person responsible for the care of others beyond the person's ability. Neglect also can occur when the person responsible for the care of an elderly person is impaired or displays unstable behavior and when the person responsible for the care of an elderly person is unable to perform minimal care tasks consistently. Examples of medical neglect include refusal or failure on the part of the person responsible for the care of an elderly person to seek, obtain, or maintain those services necessary for the person's medical, dental, and mental health needs, and withholding medically indicated treatment from elderly people.

Examples of emotional and moral neglect include failing to address the emotional needs of an elderly person and having inappropriate expectations of the person considering his or her competence and cognitive ability. Examples of self-neglect include the failure of an elderly person to eat or address his or her serious medical needs.

Services available to assist elderly people who may be experiencing abuse or neglect typically include crisis intervention, individual and family counseling, and family and caretaker education.

Eligibility Criteria

Eligibility criteria vary from program to program. Such criteria typically include evidence of abuse and neglect, social service needs, and ability to pay.

CONTACT INFORMATION

Contact state and local departments of elderly affairs, area offices on aging, senior centers, and other public and private agencies that serve elderly people.

Useful Tips

Information about abuse and neglect is available from a variety of sources.

- Children and youths:
  - o the American Humane Association (http://www.american humane.org/)
  - o Childhelp U.S.A. (http://www.childhelpusa.org/)
  - o Child Welfare Information Gateway (http://www.childwelfare.com)
  - o the Child Welfare League of America (http://www.cwla.org/)
  - o the National Youth Violence Prevention Resource Center (http://www.safeyouth.org/scripts/topics/childabuse.asp)
  - o Prevent Child Abuse America (http://www.preventchildabuse.org/)
- Developmental disabilities:
  - o Administration on Developmental Disabilities, Administration for Children and Families (http://www.acf.hhs.gov/programs/add/)
  - o National Association of Councils on Developmental Disabilities (http://www.nacdd.org/)
  - o Developmental Disabilities Online (http://www.pnsonline.org/)
  - o Disability: U.S. Government Disability Information Web site (http://www.disabilityinfo.gov)
- Women:
  - o National Domestic Violence Hotline (http://www.ndvh.org/)
  - o National Sexual Violence Resource Center (http://www.nsvrc.org/)
  - o the Office on Violence Against Women, U.S. Department of Justice (http://www.ovw.usdoj.gov/)

- o the Rape, Abuse, and Incest National Network (http://www.rainn.org/)
- o Violence Against Women, U.S. Department of Health and Human Services (http://www.4woman.gov/violence/)
- Domestic violence:
  - o Gay, Lesbian, Bisexual, and Transgendered Domestic Violence (http://www.rainbowdomesticviolence.itgo.com/)
  - o the National Center for Victims of Crime (http://www.ncvc.org/)
  - o the National Domestic Violence Hotline (http://www.ndvh.org/)
  - o the National Coalition Against Domestic Violence (http://www.ncadv.org/)
  - o the National Organization for Victim Assistance (http://www.try-nova.org/)
  - o the Office for Victims of Crime, U.S. Department of Justice (http://www.ojp.usdoj.gov/ovc)
  - o Victim Assistance Online (http://www.vaonline.org/)
- Elders:
  - o the Center of Excellence in Elder Abuse and Neglect (http://www.centeronelderabuse.org/)
  - o the Clearinghouse on Abuse and Neglect of the Elderly (http://www.cane.udel.edu/)
  - o the National Center on Elder Abuse (http://www.elderabuse-center.org/)
  - o the National Clearinghouse on Abuse in Later Life (http://www.ncall.us/)
  - o the National Committee for the Prevention of Elder Abuse (http://www.preventelderabuse.org/).

MILITARY PERSONNEL
AND VETERANS

Overview

A WIDE RANGE of social services is available to military personnel, veterans, and their families. Services and programs address issues related to health care, mental health, physical disabilities, parenting, personal crises, housing, education, substance abuse, domestic violence, legal affairs, family emergencies, and retirement.

Military Personnel

SERVICES AND BENEFITS
The major military branches offer human and social services under their respective auspices. Each branch provides services related to health care, mental health, substance abuse, domestic violence, children and youths, family emergencies, housing, finances, retirement, and legal issues to active military personnel and their families. Important examples of human services offered by the military include the following:

Department of the Army

- Army OneSource provides Army personnel and their families with 24-hour access to a toll-free information and referral hotline for assistance with personal and family challenges.
- Military OneSource provides military personnel and their families with 24-hour access to a toll-free information and referral hotline for assistance with personal and family challenges.

145

- The Army Relief Fund provides emergency financial assistance to soldiers and their dependents.
- A 24-hour counseling hotline provides crisis intervention and support.
- The Center for Health Promotion and Preventive Medicine provides preventive medicine, public health, and health promotion and awareness services.
- The Center for Substance Abuse Programs provides comprehensive prevention and treatment services.
- Child, Youth, and School Services offers social services and counseling to family members.
- The Community and Family Support Center provides family assistance and supportive services.
- Comprehensive health care is provided to Army personnel and their dependents.
- Comprehensive housing assistance is provided to Army personnel and their dependents.
- Legal services provided include legal advice from the Armed Forces Legal Assistance Office for Army personnel regarding civil matters, such as adoption, divorce, wills and estates, consumer issues, landlord–tenant issues, domestic relations, immigration and naturalization, or personal injury matters; and legal representation from the U.S. Army Trial Defense Service for soldiers charged with military criminal offenses and during criminal investigations.
- Comprehensive mental health and counseling services are provided to Army personnel and their families.
- Retirement Services include preretirement counseling and retirement counseling related to benefits and entitlements.

Department of the Navy

- The Fleet and Family Service Center provides family assistance and supportive services.
- Comprehensive health care is provided to Navy and Marine personnel and their dependents.

- Comprehensive housing assistance is provided to Navy and Marine personnel and their dependents.
- Legal services include legal advice from the Armed Forces Legal Assistance Office for Navy and Marine personnel regarding civil matters, such as adoption, consumer issues, landlord–tenant issues, domestic relations, immigration and naturalization, or personal injury matters; and legal representation through the Trial Services Offices for Navy and Marine personnel charged with military criminal offenses and during criminal investigations.
- Comprehensive mental health and counseling services are provided for Navy and Marine personnel and their families.
- Military OneSource provides military personnel and their families with 24-hour access to a toll-free information and referral hotline for assistance with personal and family challenges.
- Retirement services include preretirement counseling and retirement counseling related to benefits and entitlements.
- Substance abuse and rehabilitation services include comprehensive prevention and treatment services.

Department of the Air Force

- Air Force Crossroads provides Air Force personnel and their families with comprehensive information related to human and social services.
- Military OneSource provides military personnel and their families with 24-hour access to a toll-free information and referral hotline for assistance with personal and family challenges
- Comprehensive health care is provided to Air Force personnel and their dependents.
- Comprehensive housing assistance is provided to Air Force personnel and their dependents.
- Legal services include legal advice through the Armed Forces Legal Assistance Office for Air Force personnel regarding civil matters, such as adoption, consumer issues, landlord–tenant issues, domestic relations, immigration and naturalization, or personal injury

matters; and legal representation through the Judge Advocate General for Air Force personnel charged with military criminal offenses and during criminal investigations.

- Comprehensive mental health and counseling services are provided for Air Force personnel and their families.
- Retirement services include preretirement counseling and retirement counseling related to benefits and entitlements.
- Substance abuse and rehabilitation services include comprehensive prevention and treatment services.

Coast Guard

- The Office of Work-Life provides Coast Guard personnel and their families with comprehensive information related to human and social services.
- The Family Advocacy Program provides family assistance and supportive services.
- Comprehensive health care is provided to Coast Guard personnel and their dependents.
- Comprehensive housing assistance is provided to Coast Guard personnel and their dependents.
- Legal services include legal advice through the Armed Forces Legal Assistance program for Coast Guard personnel regarding civil matters, such as adoption, consumer issues, landlord–tenant issues, domestic relations, immigration and naturalization, or personal injury matters; and legal representation through the Judge Advocate General for Coast Guard personnel charged with military criminal offenses and during criminal investigations.
- Comprehensive mental health and counseling services are provided for Coast Guard personnel and their families.
- Military OneSource provides military personnel and their families with 24-hour access to a toll-free information and referral hotline for assistance with personal and family challenges.
- Retirement services include preretirement counseling and retirement counseling related to benefits and entitlements.

- Substance abuse and rehabilitation services include comprehensive prevention and treatment services.

ELIGIBILITY CRITERIA
The military branches have diverse eligibility criteria for their various services and programs.

CONTACT INFORMATION
Contact military social workers, medical personnel, counselors, resource specialists, and other human resources personnel.

Veterans

SERVICES AND BENEFITS
The Department of Veterans Affairs offers a wide range of human and social services. The Veterans Health Administration provides a wide range of health and social services to veterans and their families. The Veterans Benefits Administration also provides a wide range of benefits and services to veterans and their families.

Veterans Health Administration

- Readjustment counseling services for bereavement or posttraumatic stress are available at Veterans' Centers to assist returning veterans with postwar adjustment.
- Homeless veterans receive outreach, assessment, counseling, medical treatment, shelter, assistance with transitional and permanent housing, and job and educational assistance.
- Blind rehabilitation services help veterans' adjustment through blindness counseling, patient and family education, benefit analysis, residential inpatient training, outpatient rehabilitation services, and provision of assistive technology.
- HIV/AIDS prevention, treatment, and counseling services are provided.

- Cancer care includes prevention, detection, treatment, and counseling services.
- Elder care services include information and services related to hospice care, home-based primary care, geriatric evaluation and management, domiciliary care, treatment of Alzheimer's disease and dementia, adult day care, and respite care.
- Mental health and illness prevention, identification, and treatment services are provided.
- Services are provided related to women's health care, such as gynecological and cancer care, posttraumatic stress, and sexual trauma.

Veterans Benefits Administration

- Compensation and pension services include provision of comprehensive benefit information related to all Department of Veterans Affairs programs and services, covering, for example, Agent Orange, AIDS, burial, clothing allowances, compensation, disability, education, health care, posttraumatic stress, retirement, sexual trauma, survivors' benefits, transportation, vocational rehabilitation, and women's issues.
- Educational benefits and programs are provided for veterans, survivors, and dependents.
- Vocational rehabilitation and employment services assist veterans with vocational rehabilitation, independent living, vocational and educational counseling, employment searches, and job skills training.
- Survivors' and dependents' benefits are provided for surviving spouses, children, and parents of veterans.
- Burial services are provided for veterans and eligible family members.
- Medical, surgical, and rehabilitation care benefits also are provided to veterans.

ELIGIBILITY CRITERIA

The Department of Veterans Affairs has diverse eligibility criteria for its various services and programs.

CONTACT INFORMATION

Contact Department of Veterans Affairs social workers, medical personnel, counselors, resource specialists, and other human resources personnel.

Useful Tips

Centralized information about human services in the armed forces is available at Military OneSource for all military personnel and their families, at https://www.militaryonesource.com. Military OneSource information on specific topics is available:

- Abuse and neglect of children (http://www.militaryonesource. com/MOS/FindInformation/Category/Topic/Issue.aspx?IssueID =1029&TopicID=399&MaterialTypeGroupIDOpened=-1)
- ADD and ADHD (http://www.militaryonesource.com/MOS/ FindInformation/Category/Topic/Issue.aspx?IssueID=164& TopicID=39&MaterialTypeGroupIDOpened=-1)
- Addictions (http://www.militaryonesource.com/MOS/Find Information/Category.aspx?CategoryID=125)
- Adoption (http://www.militaryonesource.com/MOS/Find Information/Category/Topic.aspx?TopicID=22)
- Advocacy in the schools (http://www.militaryonesource.com/ MOS/FindInformation/Category/Topic/Issue.aspx?IssueID=64& TopicID=507&MaterialTypeGroupIDOpened=-1)
- Anger management (http://www.militaryonesource.com/MOS/ FindInformation/Category/Topic/Issue.aspx?IssueID=180& TopicID=39&MaterialTypeGroupIDOpened=-1)
- Anxiety (http://www.militaryonesource.com/MOS/Find Information/Category/Topic/Issue.aspx?IssueID=165&TopicID= 39&MaterialTypeGroupIDOpened=-1)
- Casualty assistance (http://www.militaryonesource.com/MOS/ FindInformation/Category/Topic/Issue.aspx?IssueID=1171& TopicID=423&MaterialTypeGroupIDOpened=-1)
- Child care (http://www.militaryonesource.com/MOS/Find Information/Category/Topic.aspx?TopicID=25)

- Depression (http://www.militaryonesource.com/MOS/Find Information/Category/Topic/Issue.aspx?IssueID=166&TopicID=39&MaterialTypeGroupIDOpened=-1)
- Divorce and separation (http://www.militaryonesource.com/MOS/FindInformation/Category/Topic.aspx?TopicID=500)
- Eating disorders (http://www.militaryonesource.com/MOS/Find Information/Category/Topic/Issue.aspx?IssueID=50&Topic ID=402&MaterialTypeGroupIDOpened=-1)
- Elder abuse and neglect (http://www.militaryonesource.com/MOS/FindInformation/Category/Topic/Issue.aspx?IssueID=592 &TopicID=399&MaterialTypeGroupIDOpened=-1)
- Emotional well-being (http://www.militaryonesource.com/MOS/FindInformation/Category.aspx?CategoryID=163)
- End-of-life decisions (http://www.militaryonesource.com/MOS/FindInformation/Category/Topic/Issue.aspx?IssueID=1061& TopicID=349&MaterialTypeGroupIDOpened=-1)
- Funeral planning (http://www.militaryonesource.com/MOS/FindInformation/Category/Topic/Issue.aspx?IssueID=25&Topic ID=349&MaterialTypeGroupIDOpened=-1)
- Grief and loss (http://www.militaryonesource.com/MOS/Find Information/Category/Topic/Issueaspx?IssueID=158&Topic ID=423&MaterialTypeGroupIDOpened=-1)
- Hospice (http://www.militaryonesource.com/MOS/Find Information/Category/Topic/Issue.aspx?IssueID=30&Topic ID=349&MaterialTypeGroupIDOpened=-1)
- Legal aid (http://www.militaryonesource.com/MOS/Find Information/Category.aspx?CategoryID=162)
- Mental health (http://www.militaryonesource.com/MOS/FindInformation/Category/Topic.aspx?TopicID=39)
- Mood disorders (http://www.militaryonesource.com/MOS/FindInformation/Category/Topic/Issue.aspx?IssueID=1105& TopicID=39&MaterialTypeGroupIDOpened=-1)
- Parenting skills (http://www.militaryonesource.com/MOS/FindInformation/Category/Topic.aspx?TopicID=28)

- Personality disorders (http://www.militaryonesource.com/MOS/
  FindInformation/Category/Topic/Issue.aspx?IssueID=1113&
  TopicID=39&MaterialTypeGroupIDOpened=-1)
- Relationship issues (http://www.militaryonesource.com/MOS/
  FindInformation/Category/Topic.aspx?TopicID=514)
- Senior health (http://www.militaryonesource.com/MOS/Find
  Information/Category.aspx?CategoryID=148)
- Sexual assault (http://www.militaryonesource.com/MOS/Find
  Information/Category/Topic/Issue.aspx?IssueID=1183&TopicID
  =503&MaterialTypeGroupIDOpened=-1)
- Suicide (http://www.militaryonesource.com/MOS/Find
  Information/Category/Topic/Issue.aspx?IssueID=152&Topic
  ID=504&MaterialTypeGroupIDOpened=-1)
- Survivor/widow (http://www.militaryonesource.com/MOS/
  FindInformation/Category.aspx?CategoryID=154)
- Violence and trauma (http://www.militaryonesource.com/MOS/
  FindInformation/Category/Topic/Issue.aspx?IssueID=155&
  TopicID=503&MaterialTypeGroupIDOpened=-1)

General information about veterans benefits and issues is available from the U.S. Department of Veterans Affairs, at http://www.va.gov/. Information on specific topics is available:

- Health care services (http://www1.va.gov/health/)
  o Agent Orange (http://www1.va.gov/agentorange/)
  o Blind rehabilitation service (http://www1.va.gov/blindrehab/)
  o Cancer program (http://www1.va.gov/cancer/)
  o Center for Women Veterans (http://www1.va.gov/womenvet/)
  o Geriatrics and extended care (http://www1.va.gov/geriatricsshg/)
  o Gulf War veterans' illnesses (http://www1.va.gov/gulfwar/)
  o Hepatitis C (http://www.hepatitis.va.gov/)
  o HIV/AIDS (http://www.hiv.va.gov/)
  o Homeless veterans (http://www1.va.gov/homeless/)
  o Mental health (http://www.mentalhealth.va.gov/)
  o Posttraumatic stress (http://www.ncptsd.va.gov/)

- o Polytrauma services (http://www.polytrauma.va.gov/)
- o Prosthetics and sensory aids (http://www.prosthetics.va.gov/)
- Health benefits (http://www.vba.va.gov/VBA/)
  - o Burial and memorials (http://www.cem.va.gov/)
  - o Education (http://www.gibill.va.gov/)
  - o Compensation and pension (http://www.vba.va.gov/bln/21/index.htm)
  - o Home loans (http://www.homeloans.va.gov/)
  - o Life insurance (http://www.insurance.va.gov/miscellaneous/index.htm)
  - o Survivors' benefits (http://www.vba.va.gov/survivors/index.htm)
  - o Vocational rehabilitation and employment (http://www.vba.va.gov/bln/vre/index.htm)

IMMIGRANTS AND REFUGEES

Overview

IMMIGRANTS TO THE United States and refugees (people who are fleeing persecution or are afraid to return their country of origin) often need assistance with issues related to income and other financial challenges, health care, mental health, employment, physical disabilities, personal crises, housing, education, transportation, legal affairs, and family emergencies. Many federal, state, and local government agencies and private national and local organizations offer programs related to refugee resettlement and immigration.

Refugee Resettlement

SERVICES AND BENEFITS

Refugee resettlement programs help refugees become self-sufficient, learn to speak English, develop and refine job skills, understand immigration status and the citizenship process, acculturate to the United States while preserving their home cultures as much as possible, access transportation services, and access health and mental health care. Public and private refugee resettlement programs provide

- a welcome to refugees at airports and initial essential services, such as housing, clothing, food, and referrals to medical and social services
- cash assistance

- employment services, such as skills training, job development, orientation to the workplace, and job counseling
- English tutoring
- foster care for unaccompanied minors
- health benefits and health care
- information about refugee status
- mentoring services
- naturalization and citizenship services and regulations
- retirement and disability services
- services for victims of torture
- social services, including housing, furniture, food, clothing, and counseling
- translation services
- transportation services.

Eligibility Criteria

Eligibility criteria vary from program to program. Such criteria typically include refugee status, family composition, income, assets, and social service needs.

Contact Information

Each state participating in the national refugee resettlement program has a state refugee coordinator housed in the state's department of human services or in a private agency that contracts with the state to provide services to refugees. Contact the state office or private social service agencies that also provide assistance to refugees.

Immigration Services

Services and Benefits

The federal government, state governments, and many private agencies provide a variety of services to immigrants to the United States, including

- a welcome to immigrants at airports and initial essential services, such as housing, furniture, clothing, food, and referrals to medical and social services

- cash assistance
- employment assistance, such as skills training, job development, orientation to the workplace, and job counseling
- English tutoring
- foster care for unaccompanied minors
- health benefits and health care
- information about the immigration process
- mentoring services
- naturalization and citizenship services and regulations
- retirement and disability services
- social services, such as housing, food, clothing, and counseling
- translation services.

ELIGIBILITY CRITERIA

Eligibility criteria vary from program to program. Criteria typically include immigration status, family composition, income, assets, and social service needs.

CONTACT INFORMATION

Contact state and local human service agencies, such as the department of human services and private social service agencies that provide assistance to immigrants.

Useful Tips

General information about refugee resettlement is available from the Office of Refugee Resettlement, Administration for Children and Families, U.S. Department of Health and Human Services, at http://www. acf.hhs.gov/programs/orr/. The Office of Refugee Resettlement offers a wide range of information on specific topics:

- Cash and medical assistance (http://www.acf.hhs.gov/programs/ orr/programs/cma.htm)
- Human trafficking (http://www.acf.hhs.gov/trafficking/)
- Mutual assistance associations (http://www.acf.hhs.gov/ programs/orr/partners/maas.htm)

- Repatriation (http://www.acf.hhs.gov/programs/orr/programs/repatriation.htm)
- Services for older refugees (http://www.acf.hhs.gov/programs/orr/programs/services_older_ref.htm)
- Services for survivors of torture (http://www.acf.hhs.gov/programs/orr/programs/services_survivors_torture.htm)
- Unaccompanied children's services (http://www.acf.hhs.gov/programs/orr/programs/unaccompanied_alien_children.htm)
- Unaccompanied refugee minors (http://www.acf.hhs.gov/programs/orr/programs/unaccompanied_refugee_minors.htm)
- Unanticipated arrivals (http://www.acf.hhs.gov/programs/orr/programs/unanticipated_arrivals_prg.htm)

General information about immigration and immigration services is available from

- Citizenship and Immigration Services, U.S. Department of Homeland Security (http://uscis.gov/)
- the National Immigration Forum (http://www.immigrationforum.org).

Several private organizations provide assistance to, and information about, refugees and immigrants. Such organizations include

- the Church World Service (http://www.churchworldservice.org)
- Episcopal Migration Ministries (http://www.ecusa.anglican.org/emm/)
- the Ethiopian Community Development Council (http://www.ecdcinternational.org/)
- the Hebrew Immigrant Aid Society (http://www.hias.org)
- the International Organization for Migration (http://www.iom.int/#)
- the International Rescue Committee (http://www.theirc.org/)
- the Lutheran Immigration and Refugee Service (http://www.lirs.org/)
- the United Nations High Commissioner for Refugees (http://www.unhcr.org/cgi-bin/texis/vtx/home)

- the United States Conference of Catholic Bishops (http://www.nccbuscc.org/mrs/)
- the U.S. Committee for Refugees and Immigrants (http://www.refugees.org/)
- World Relief Refugee Services (http://www.wr.org/).

EDUCATION AND LITERACY

Overview

A NUMBER OF educational programs and services are available to people who want to enhance their education or address unique educational needs. These programs pertain to early childhood education, special education, adult basic education and literacy education, the Upward Bound Program, vocational education, distance education, and the Federal Work–Study Program.

Early Childhood Education

SERVICES AND BENEFITS
Early childhood education programs are provided by child care centers, preschools, and school-age child care programs. Early childhood education programs are designed to promote and enhance young children's awareness, curiosity, exploration, self-esteem, problem-solving skills, independence, social skills, language and communication skills, motor skills, cognitive skills, visual and auditory skills, basic academic skills, and health habits.

ELIGIBILITY CRITERIA
Admission to early childhood education programs usually is based on students' age, educational status, and special needs. Some subsidized programs consider family income.

161

Contact state and local departments of education and school districts.

Special Education

SERVICES AND BENEFITS
Special education programs include specially designed instruction to meet the needs of children who have behavioral, emotional, physical, or psychiatric disabilities. Special education is provided through a con-tinuum of services that includes instruction using assistive technology, resource material and assistance, specially equipped classrooms, instruc-tion in a special school, home-based instruction, and instruction in hos-pitals and institutions. Traditional disability categories include autism, emotional impairment, hearing impairments, mental retardation, ortho-pedic impairments, pervasive developmental disorders, speech and lan-guage impairments, traumatic brain injury, visual impairments, and other developmental delays.

ELIGIBILITY CRITERIA
Eligibility criteria vary among special education programs. Criteria typi-cally include students' age, educational status, and disability.

CONTACT INFORMATION
Contact state and local departments of education and individual public and private schools.

Adult Basic Education, General Education Development, and Literacy Programs

SERVICES AND BENEFITS
Adult basic education programs help adults become literate, complete their secondary school education, obtain knowledge and skills required to obtain and sustain employment, and obtain the knowledge and skills required to support their children's education. Learning activities focus on arithmetic, listening and speaking, problem-solving skills, and reading

and writing. Prominent programs include Adult Basic Education (ABE), General Educational Development (GED), and the federal Project Even Start. ABE provides instruction in the basic skills of reading, writing, and mathematics to adult learners to prepare them for transitioning into the labor market or higher academic or vocational training. The GED program provides students with a high school equivalency diploma. Project Even Start (Even Start Family Literacy Program) promotes literacy among members of low-income families.

ELIGIBILITY CRITERIA
Typical eligibility criteria include age and academic standing.

CONTACT INFORMATION
Contact state and local departments of education, school districts, and independent agencies that sponsor literacy education.

Upward Bound

SERVICES AND BENEFITS
The goal of Upward Bound is to increase the rates at which participants enroll in and graduate from institutions of postsecondary education. Sponsored by colleges and universities, the program provides instruction in foreign languages, literature, laboratory science, and mathematics. Upward Bound also provides

- academic, financial, and personal counseling
- assistance in completing college entrance and financial aid applications
- assistance in preparing for college entrance examinations
- exposure to academic programs and cultural events
- information on postsecondary education opportunities
- instruction in reading, writing, study skills, and other subjects necessary for success in education beyond high school
- mentoring programs
- tutorial services

- work–study positions to expose participants to careers requiring a postsecondary degree.

ELIGIBILITY CRITERIA
Upward Bound serves high school students from low-income families; high school students from families in which neither parent holds a bachelor's degree; and low-income, first-generation military veterans who are planning to enter postsecondary education.

CONTACT INFORMATION
Contact institutions of higher education, local education agencies, non-profit organizations, and state education agencies that sponsor the program.

Vocational Education

SERVICES AND BENEFITS
Vocational education programs provide career and job-related knowledge and skills. They are offered in various educational settings, such as adult education programs, community colleges, and vocational and technical high schools.

ELIGIBILITY CRITERIA
Eligibility criteria vary among programs. Criteria typically include academic standing and background.

CONTACT INFORMATION
Contact state and local departments of education, departments of labor, school districts, and educational institutions that sponsor vocational education.

Distance Education

SERVICES AND BENEFITS
Through audio, video, and computer technology, distance education provides instruction to students who are not physically present in the same

location as the instructor. Common distance education techniques make use of

- data technology, through computer conferencing, e-mail, and facsimile
- video technology, through videoconferencing and two-way television
- voice technology, through audioconferencing, shortwave radio, the telephone, and tapes.

ELIGIBILITY CRITERIA
Eligibility criteria vary among distance education programs. Admissions criteria typically include academic standing and background.

CONTACT INFORMATION
Contact colleges, universities, and other educational organizations that sponsor distance education courses and degree programs.

Federal Work–Study Program

SERVICES AND BENEFITS
The Federal Work–Study Program provides jobs for undergraduate, graduate, and vocational students with financial need attending eligible postsecondary institutions.

ELIGIBILITY CRITERIA
Eligibility is based on financial need and academic standing.

CONTACT INFORMATION
Contact the work–study offices at postsecondary institutions of higher learning.

Useful Tips

General information about educational programs and services is available from the U.S. Department of Education (http://www.ed.gov).

Sources of information about early childhood education programs include

- the Association for Childhood Education International (http://www.acei.org/)
- the Council for Exceptional Children (http://www.cec.sped.org/)
- the National Association for the Education of Young Children (http://www.naeyc.org/)
- the National Association of Child Care Resource and Referral Agencies (http://www.naccrra.org/)
- the National Child Care Association (http://www.nccanet.org/)
- the National Child Care Information Center, U.S. Department of Health and Human Services (http://www.nccic.org/)
- the National Early Childhood Program Accreditation (http://www.necpa.net)
- the U.S. Department of Education (http://www.ed.gov/parents/earlychild/ready/resources.html).

Sources of information about special education include

- the National Association of Private Special Education Centers (http://www.napsec.org/)
- the National Association of State Directors of Special Education (http://www.nasdse.org/)
- the National Dissemination Center for Children with Disabilities (http://www.nichcy.org/)
- the Transition Coalition (http://www.transitioncoalition.org/)
- the U.S. Department of Education (http://www.ed.gov/about/offices/list/osers/osep/index.html).

Sources of information about adult basic education and literacy programs include

- the Adult Literacy and Technology Network (http://www.altn.org/)
- Bridges to the Future Initiative (http://www.literacy.org/Projects/BFI/)

- Captured Wisdom (http://www.literacy.org/HTMs/project_capturedwisdom.htm)
- the Center for Literacy Studies (http://cls.coe.utk.edu/)
- the Center for the Study of Adult Literacy (http://education.gsu.edu/csal/)
- the Early Childhood Education Network (http://www.literacycenter.net/)
- Even Start program, U.S. Department of Education (http://www.ed.gov/programs/evenstartformula/index.html)
- International Literacy Explorer (http://www.literacy.org/Projects/explorer/index.html)
- Learning Connections (http://www.literacy.org/HTMs/project_learningconnections.htm)
- the Lindy Boggs National Center for Community Literacy (http://www.boggslit.org/)
- literacy.org—online information from the University of Pennsylvania (http://www.literacy.org/)
- the National Center for Family Literacy (http://www.famlit.org/)
- the National Center for the Study of Adult Learning and Literacy (http://gseweb.harvard.edu/~ncsall/)
- the National Institute for Literacy (http://www.nifl.gov/)
- the National LINCS—online information from the National Institute for Literacy (http://www.nifl.gov/lincs/)
- Office of Vocational and Adult Education, U.S. Department of Education (http://www.ed.gov/about/offices/list/ovae/pi/AdultEd/index.html)
- ProLiteracy (http://www.proliteracy.org/)
- Tech21 (http://www.literacy.org/HTMs/project_tech21.htm).

Information about Upward Bound is available from the U.S. Department of Education at http://www.ed.gov/programs/trioupbound/.

Sources of information about career and vocational education include

- America's Career Resource Network (http://www.acrnetwork.org/)

- the Association for Career and Technical Education (http://www.acteonline.org/)
- the Career Academy Support Network (http://casn.berkeley.edu/)
- the International Vocational Education and Training Association (http://www.iveta.org/)
- the International Technology Education Association (http://www.iteaconnect.org/)
- the National Academy Foundation (http://www.naf.org/)
- the National Association of State Directors of Career Technical Education Consortium (http://www.careertech.org/)
- National Centers for Career and Technical Education (http://www.nccte.com/)
- Office of Vocational and Adult Education, U.S. Department of Education (http://www.ed.gov/about/offices/list/ovae/).

Sources of information about distance education include

- the American Distance Education Consortium (http://www.adec.edu/)
- the Distance Education and Training Council (http://www.detc.org/)
- the Distance Education Clearinghouse (http://www.uwex.edu/disted/index.cfm)
- Online Education Resources (http://www.ion.illinois.edu/resources/)
- the United States Distance Learning Association (http://www.usdla.org/)
- the World Association for Online Education (http://www.waoe.org/).

Information about the Federal Work–Study Program is available from the U.S. Department of Education at http://www.ed.gov/programs/fws/.

EMPLOYMENT ASSISTANCE

Overview

PEOPLE SOMETIMES NEED help finding and maintaining employment. Sometimes people need to learn new skills to be qualified for a new job. Several employment and labor programs are available that can help people with these job-related issues. They include programs to help people find jobs, train for a new job, get help when they experience problems at work, and cope with unemployment.

Seeking Employment

SERVICES AND BENEFITS

Many programs are available to help people find jobs. Employment programs are designed to help people enhance their job-seeking skills related to the following core skills:

- locating job search guides
- evaluating labor market and employment trends
- networking
- designing a resume and cover letter
- completing job applications
- interviewing
- evaluating a job offer
- negotiating for salary and benefits.

ELIGIBILITY CRITERIA
Eligibility criteria vary among employment assistance programs. Criteria typically include educational background, work experience, and work-related skills.

CONTACT INFORMATION
Contact state and local departments of labor and training, vocational education and training programs, unemployment offices, and private employment consulting and search firms.

Job Training

SERVICES AND BENEFITS
Job training programs help people acquire the knowledge and skills they need to obtain employment or train for a new field or career. Job training programs focus on

- career advancement strategies and tools
- essential job-related knowledge and skills
- work habits, such as appearance, attendance, initiative, punctuality, social and interpersonal skills, and work quality.

ELIGIBILITY CRITERIA
Eligibility criteria vary among job training programs. Criteria typically include educational background, work experience, and work-related skills.

CONTACT INFORMATION
Contact state and local departments of labor and training, vocational education and training programs, unemployment offices, and private job training programs.

Employee Assistance

SERVICES AND BENEFITS
Employees sometimes encounter challenges in the workplace. Common problems include experiencing significant stress, having conflict with

colleagues, struggling with substance abuse problems, or feeling harassed by supervisors. Employees sometimes feel the need for help with these problems. Employers and supervisors sometimes insist that employees get help when they believe that the employees' problems are affecting their work.

Many employers sponsor employee assistance programs (EAPs) to help employees who are experiencing work-related problems and stress as a result of emotional problems, employee conflict, family responsibilities and stress, financial and legal problems, substance abuse, or workplace stress. EAPs typically provide short-term counseling to employees and, when necessary, referrals to mental health professionals and social service programs for longer term assistance. EAPs ordinarily provide

- assessments of fitness for duty
- assessments of issues related to mental health, substance abuse, workplace challenges, and other personal problems
- referrals for long-term counseling and treatment
- short-term counseling for individuals, couples, and families
- telephone access for employees and family members to professional counselors for assessment, consultation, referral, and crisis intervention.

ELIGIBILITY CRITERIA
Eligibility criteria vary among EAPs. Criteria typically include employee status, reason for referral, and employee benefits.

CONTACT INFORMATION
Contact employers' personnel and human resources offices for information about available EAP services.

Coping with Unemployment

SERVICES AND BENEFITS
Coping with unemployment can be very difficult. Unemployed workers need information about unemployment benefits and services designed to

help workers find new employment. Unemployment insurance ordinarily provides benefits to workers who are out of work through no fault of their own. Unemployment counseling, which is sometimes called outplacement counseling, provides former employees with career counseling, coaching, and workshops to help them find new employment and train for new jobs.

ELIGIBILITY CRITERIA

Eligibility criteria vary among employers and the unemployment programs sponsored by government agencies. Unemployment insurance benefits are based on prior earnings and the reasons for unemployment.

CONTACT INFORMATION

Contact state and local unemployment offices and employers' personnel and human resources offices.

Useful Tips

Information and advice about seeking employment are widely available. Particularly useful organizations and resources include

- America's Job Bank (http://www.ajb.org/)
- Career InfoNet (http://www.acinet.org/acinet/)
- Career One Stop (http://www.careeronestop.org/)
- the Career Resource Library (http://www.acinet.org/acinet/crl/library.aspx)
- Career Voyages, U.S. Department of Labor and U.S. Department of Education (http://www.careervoyages.gov/)
- the O*Net Computerized Interest Profiler (http://www.onet center.org/CIP.html)
- the O*Net Work Importance Profiler (http://www.onetcenter.org/WIP.html)
- USAJOBS (http://www.usajobs.opm.gov/).

Sources of information on job training include

- the Association for Career and Technical Education (http://www.acteonline.org/)
- the Employment and Training Administration, U.S. Department of Labor (http://www.doleta.gov/)
- Job Corps (http://jobcorps.doleta.gov/)
- the Office of Apprenticeship Training, Employment and Training Administration (http://www.doleta.gov/atels_bat/)
- Workforce Tools of the Trade (http://www.workforcetools.org/)
- Workforce3 One (http://www.workforce3one.org/).

Information about coping with workplace challenges is available from the Employee Assistance Professionals Association at http://www.eapassn.org/.

Sources of information about unemployment assistance and outplacement counseling is available from

- the Association of Career Management Consulting Firms International (http://www.aocfi.org/)
- Career One Stop (http://www.careeronestop.org/)
- the Employment and Training Administration (http://ows.doleta.gov/unemploy/ and http://www.doleta.gov/layoff/workers.cfm)
- Self-employment assistance (http://www.workforcesecurity.doleta.gov/unemploy/self.asp)
- State rapid response coordinators (http://www.doleta.gov/layoff/rapid_coord.cfm)
- Unemployment insurance (http://www.workforcesecurity.doleta.gov/unemploy/aboutui.asp).

AGING AND RETIREMENT: FINANCIAL AND LEGAL ISSUES

Overview

GROWING OLDER POSES many challenges. People face many health care–related issues, such as coping with disabilities, nursing home placement, hospice, end-of-life decisions, and so on. The processes of aging and retirement also present challenging financial and legal issues. Important issues may arise concerning retirement income, estate planning, trusts, and wills.

Retirement Income

SERVICES AND BENEFITS

People who are planning for retirement should address several issues related to income. Many retirement-planning professionals and tools are available to help people assess their income needs and resources. Retirement planners will advise a consumer to consider

- current age
- current annual income
- desired postretirement annual income
- desired retirement age
- expected annual pension
- expected social security income
- income from investments and savings, such as annuities, individual retirement accounts, stocks, bonds, and certificates of deposit
- life expectancy.

Services and advisors are available to anyone interested in retirement planning. Many online retirement calculators are available without charge. Many financial advisors offer retirement planning for a fee.

Considerable information about retirement planning is available from financial institutions, such as banks, mutual funds, and insurance companies, and from advisors with appropriate credentials.

Estate Planning

Many people wish to make plans for the distribution of their assets after their death. The purpose of estate planning is to arrange the distribution of assets to beneficiaries quickly and with minimal tax consequences. The process of estate planning involves conducting an inventory of assets and making a will, establishing a trust, or both. A will is a written document that directs how a person's assets and possessions are to be distributed at the time of death. A trust is a legal entity or device used to take care of property in special ways. A trust is created by a legal agreement between two parties, called the grantor and the trustee.

The inventory of assets for estate planning includes

- residence
- other real estate
- savings, such as bank accounts, certificates of deposit, or money market accounts
- investments, such as stocks, bonds, or mutual funds
- pension and retirement accounts
- life insurance policies and annuities
- ownership interest in a business
- motor vehicles, including automobiles, boats, and planes
- jewelry
- other personal property.

A trust functions primarily to

- avoid probate (the process of officially proving the validity of a will)
- control the transfer of the estate to heirs
- manage an estate during mental incapacitation
- protect the estate from lawsuits and seizures
- reduce or eliminate estate taxes.

Examples of trusts include

- bypass trusts, which are irrevocable trusts that allow the passing of a person's assets to his or her children to reduce estate taxes;
- living trusts, which are created for a person and administered by someone else while that person is still alive, thus avoiding probate and therefore resulting in a quicker distribution of assets;
- life insurance trusts, which are set up to buy life insurance coverage or to become the owners of an existing policy because the death benefit is not counted as part of the insured person's estate for tax purposes;
- charitable remainder trusts, in which property or money is donated to a charity but the donor continues to use the property, receive income from the property, or both until his or her death, thus minimizing capital gains taxes and estate taxes.

ELIGIBILITY CRITERIA
Estate planning services are available to any interested person. Attorneys charge fees to assist with estate planning.

CONTACT INFORMATION
Contact attorneys who specialize in trusts and estates.

Useful Tips

Several organizations provide information about financial consultants and advisors. Those organizations include

- the American Academy of Financial Management (http://www. financialcertified.com/)

- the American Institute of Certified Public Accountants (https://www.aicpa.org)
- the Certified Financial Planner Board of Standards (http://www.cfp.net)
- the Financial Planning Association (http://www.fpanet.org/)
- the International Association for Registered Financial Planners (http://www.iarfc.org/)
- the National Association of Financial and Estate Planning (http://www.nafep.com/)
- the Society of Certified Senior Advisors (http://www.csa-csa.com/).

For information about social security benefits, contact the Social Security Administration (http://www.ssa.gov/).

For information about estate planning, contact

- the American Academy of Estate Planning Attorneys (http://www.aaepa.com/)
- the American College of Trust and Estate Counsel (http://www.actec.org/)
- the National Academy of Elder Law Attorneys (http://www.naela.org/)
- the National Association of Estate Planners and Councils (http://www.naepc.org/estate_planners.web)
- the National Association of Financial and Estate Planning (http://www.nafep.com/)
- the National Elder Law Foundation (http://www.nelf.org/)
- the National Network of Estate Planning Attorneys (http://www.netplanning.com/).

LEGAL SERVICES AND DISPUTE RESOLUTION

Overview

PEOPLE OFTEN NEED legal advice and services. Common legal issues concern

- adoption
- bankruptcy
- business transactions
- child custody or support
- civil rights
- contracts
- criminal defense
- divorce
- education
- estate planning
- finances
- health care
- immigration
- labor
- landlord–tenant relationships
- litigation
- malpractice
- personal injury
- product liability

- real estate
- sexual harassment
- social security
- taxation
- traffic violations
- workers' compensation.

Most people pay fees to obtain legal advice and services from private attorneys. Some people are eligible for low-cost or no-cost legal advice and services from legal aid offices, legal clinics, and public defenders.

Many people involved in disputes with employers, business associates, neighbors, spouses, or partners prefer to avoid formal court proceedings. These parties have the option to participate in arbitration and mediation, alternative forms of dispute resolution, in an effort to resolve their disagreements.

Legal Aid

Services and Benefits
Legal aid offices provide legal services to low-income people concerning a variety of civil (noncriminal) matters. Legal issues commonly addressed by legal aid offices include adoption; child custody; child support; consumer fraud; disability; divorce; domestic violence; education; employment; health; housing; labor; and public benefits, such as welfare and other forms of public assistance.

Eligibility Criteria
Eligibility for legal aid services ordinarily is based on income and the nature of the legal issue.

Contact Information
Contact state or local bar association offices to find out about local legal aid offices and clinics. Legal aid clinics may be freestanding or sponsored by a law school.

Public Defenders

SERVICES AND BENEFITS
Public defenders are lawyers who provide free criminal defense services to indigent individuals who have been charged with a crime.

ELIGIBILITY CRITERIA
Eligibility to receive public defender services ordinarily is based on income and evidence of indigence.

CONTACT INFORMATION
Contact the public defender's office affiliated with the federal, state, or local court.

Dispute Resolution: Arbitration and Mediation

SERVICES AND BENEFITS
Arbitration and mediation services offer a means of resolving disputes between parties without going to court. Arbitration is the submission of a dispute to one or more impartial persons for a final and binding decision. Through contractual agreements, participating parties may control the range of issues to be resolved, the types of possible relief, and many procedural aspects of the process.

Mediation is a process in which a neutral party assists disputing parties in reaching their own settlement but does not have the authority to make a binding decision. In some situations participating parties may agree to combine mediation and arbitration. In these situations a neutral party serves as both mediator and arbitrator. The neutral party then attempts to mediate a dispute and, when necessary, has the authority to issue a final and binding decision.

ELIGIBILITY CRITERIA
Mediation and arbitration require the participants' agreement and willingness to participate in the process.

CONTACT INFORMATION

Contact potential mediators and arbitrators through the American Arbitration Association and other national and local directories.

Useful Tips

For information about legal aid services, contact

- the Legal Services Corporation (http://www.lsc.gov)
- the National Legal Aid and Defender Association (http://www.nlada.org/).

For information about locating attorneys and obtaining referrals for legal services, contact the American Bar Association and local lawyer referral services (http://www.abanet.org/legalservices/lris/directory/).

For information about mediation and arbitration services, contact

- the Alternative Dispute Resolution Resource Guide, National Center for State Courts (http://www.ncsconline.org/WC/CourTopics/ResourceGuide.asp?topic=ADRMed)
- the American Arbitration Association (http://www.adr.org)
- the Association of Attorney-Mediators (http://www.attorney-mediators.org/)
- the Association for Conflict Resolution (http://www.acrnet.org/)
- the Association of Family and Conciliation Courts (http://www.afccnet.org/)
- the Center for Resolution (http://www.centerforresolution.com/)
- the Center for Restorative Justice and Peacemaking (http://cehd.umn.edu/ssw/rjp/)
- the Centre for Restorative Justice (http://www.sfu.ca/cfrj/about.html)
- the National Association for Community Mediation (http://www.nafcm.org/)

- the National Institute for Advanced Conflict Resolution (http://www.niacr.org/)
- the Straus Institute for Dispute Resolution, Pepperdine University School of Law (http://www.mediate.com/)
- the Victim–Offender Mediation Association (http://www.voma.org/).

CRIME VICTIMS SERVICES

Overview

VICTIM ASSISTANCE PROGRAMS offer a wide range of services to crime victims. The victim assistance movement began in the early 1970s as a result of growing recognition that crime victims often need assistance to help them cope with their traumatic experiences. Many crime victims face mental health challenges; they may develop disabling anxiety or become severely depressed, for example. In addition, some crime victims suffer financial harm as a result of crimes such as robbery, burglary, or larceny.

Victim assistance programs typically employ staffers who are trained to understand victimization and provide clinical and other supportive services. Training may focus on

- history of the victim services field
- victims' rights and the justice system
- impact of crime on victims
- communicating with victims and survivors
- providing direct services to victims and survivors
- collaborating for victims' rights and services
- cultural and spiritual competence
- ethics in victim services
- developing resilience
- personal attitudes, biases, and beliefs and their impact on responses to victims of crime

185

- understanding the prevalence and symptoms of compassion fatigue and vicarious trauma
- the impact of traumatic stress and fear on victim services professionals.

SERVICES AND BENEFITS

Many communities offer comprehensive services to crime victims, including victims of sexual assault and molestation, assault and battery, arson, kidnapping, domestic violence, neglect, driving under the influence, hit and run, gang violence, financial fraud and exploitation, hate and bias crime, dating violence, human trafficking, identity theft, robbery, larceny, burglary, stalking, terrorism, and murder (survivors). Services may include information and referral, assistance in filing victims compensation claims, crisis counseling, psychotherapy, emergency financial assistance, personal and legal advocacy, forensic examinations, fraud investigation, emergency shelter, supervised visitation, transportation, support groups, victim–offender mediation, and legal services.

Victim services typically address psychological, physical, and financial harm. Physical injuries may include the following: physiological anxiety; gunshot wounds, lacerations, broken bones, sprains, or burns; physical injuries that lead to other health conditions, such as heart attack, stroke, fractures from falling, loss of dexterity; increased risk of cardiac distress, irritable bowel syndrome, or chronic pain; permanent disability; disfigurement; immune disorders that increase potential for infectious diseases; substantial lifestyle changes, including restriction of activities once enjoyed; lethargy and body fatigue; sleep disorders; loss of appetite, excessive appetite, or eating disorders; decreased libido and sexual dysfunction; inability to work. For sexual assault victims, injuries may include possible exposure to sexually transmitted infections, exposure to HIV, or unwanted pregnancy.

Typical psychological injuries include shock, terror, feelings of unreality, feelings of numbness, confusion, self-blame, inability to concentrate, helplessness, fear, anger and rage, grief or intense sorrow, anxiety, shame, panic symptoms, difficulty trusting oneself or others, depression, increased risk of alcohol or drug abuse, concern about future victimization, feelings of vulnerability, social withdrawal and isolation, problems in personal and intimate relationships, and suicidal ideation.

ELIGIBILITY CRITERIA
Common eligibility criteria include evidence of victimization and injury.

CONTACT INFORMATION
Information about local crime victims programs can be obtained from local prosecutors' offices and agencies that administer crime victims programs. The U.S. Department of Justice, Office for Victims of Crimes, sponsors an online search service to help people locate local programs (http://ovc.ncjrs.gov/findvictimservices/).

Useful Tips

Information is available about a number of specific victim populations and services that may be helpful to them:

- American Indians (http://www.ojp.usdoj.gov/ovc/help/ai.htm)
- Campus crime (http://www.ojp.usdoj.gov/ovc/help/cc.htm)
- Child abuse (http://www.ojp.usdoj.gov/ovc/help/ca.htm)
- Civil legal remedies (http://www.ojp.usdoj.gov/ovc/help/civil. htm)
- Crime victims' rights (http://www.ojp.usdoj.gov/ovc/help/cvr.htm)
- Dating violence (http://www.ojp.usdoj.gov/ovc/help/date violence.htm)
- Domestic violence (http://www.ojp.usdoj.gov/ovc/help/dv.htm)
- Driving under the influence (http://www.ojp.usdoj.gov/ovc/ help/dd.htm)
- Elder abuse (http://www.ojp.usdoj.gov/ovc/help/ea.htm)
- Fraud and identity theft (http://www.ojp.usdoj.gov/ovc/help/ it.htm)
- Hate and bias crimes (http://www.ojp.usdoj.gov/ovc/help/hbc. htm)

- Homicide survivors (http://www.ojp.usdoj.gov/ovc/help/hv.htm)
- Incest and sexual abuse (http://www.ojp.usdoj.gov/ovc/help/isa.htm)
- Military victims (http://www.ojp.usdoj.gov/ovc/help/military.htm)
- Missing and exploited children (http://www.ojp.usdoj.gov/ovc/help/mec.htm)
- Physical assault (http://www.ojp.usdoj.gov/ovc/help/pa.htm)
- Posttraumatic stress disorder (http://www.ojp.usdoj.gov/ovc/help/ptsd.htm)
- Sexual assault and rape (http://www.ojp.usdoj.gov/ovc/help/rape.htm)
- Stalking (http://www.ojp.usdoj.gov/ovc/help/stalk.htm)
- Terrorism and mass violence (http://www.ojp.usdoj.gov/ovc/help/terrorism.htm)
- Trafficking in persons (http://www.ojp.usdoj.gov/ovc/help/tip.htm)
- Victims with disabilities (http://www.ojp.usdoj.gov/ovc/help/disabled.htm)
- Workplace violence (http://www.ojp.usdoj.gov/ovc/help/workviol.htm)

DISASTER ASSISTANCE

Overview

DISASTERS ARE AN unfortunate fact of life. Tornadoes, hurricanes, explosions, floods, earthquakes, fires, hazardous spills, landslides, terrorism, and other natural and human-made disasters create enormous problems. People's lives can be turned upside down in an instant, creating sudden demand for shelter, health care, food, and clothing. In addition to the demand for these necessities, disaster victims face compelling emotional challenges as a result of the death of loved ones, serious injury, and other trauma.

SERVICES AND BENEFITS

At the national level, the Federal Emergency Management Agency (FEMA) offers a wide range of services. FEMA is headquartered in Washington, DC, and operates regional and area offices across the country, the Mount Weather Emergency Operations Center, and the National Emergency Training Center in Maryland. FEMA also has standby disaster assistance employees who are available for deployment after disasters. Often FEMA works in partnership with other organizations that are part of the nation's emergency management system. These partners include state and local emergency management agencies, 27 federal agencies, and the American Red Cross.

FEMA oversees the National Incident Management System (NIMS). The NIMS provides a systematic approach to guide departments and agencies at all levels of government, nongovernmental organizations, and the private sector to prevent, protect against, respond to, recover from, and mitigate the effects of incidents, regardless of cause, size, location, or complexity, to reduce the loss of life and property and harm to the environment.

NIMS works with the National Response Framework (NRF). NIMS provides the template for the management of incidents; NRF provides the structure and mechanisms for national-level policy for incident management. The NRF presents the guiding principles that enable response partners to prepare for and provide a unified national response to disasters and emergencies. It establishes a comprehensive, national, all-hazards approach to domestic incident response.

The NRF

- describes how communities, tribes, states, the federal government, private-sector organizations, and nongovernmental partners work together to coordinate national response
- describes specific authorities and best practices for managing incidents
- builds on the NIMS, which provides a consistent template for managing incidents.

According to current national guidelines, first response to a disaster is the job of local governments' emergency services, with help from nearby municipalities, the state, and volunteer agencies. In a catastrophic disaster, and if a state's governor requests, federal resources can be mobilized through FEMA for search and rescue, electrical power, food, water, shelter, and other basic human needs.

A major disaster could result from a hurricane, earthquake, flood, tornado, or major fire, which the president determines warrants supplemental federal aid. The event must be clearly more than state or local governments can handle alone. If a disaster is declared, funding comes from the President's Disaster Relief Fund, which is managed by FEMA, and disaster aid programs of other participating federal agencies. A Presidential Major Disaster Declaration (MDD) puts into motion long-term federal recovery programs, some of which are matched by state programs and are designed to help disaster victims, businesses, and public entities.

An Emergency Declaration is more limited in scope and without the long-term federal recovery programs of an MDD. Generally, federal assistance and funding are provided to meet a specific emergency need or to help prevent a major disaster from occurring. An MDD usually follows these steps:

- Local government responds, supplemented by neighboring communities and volunteer agencies.
- The state responds with state resources, such as the National Guard and state agencies.
- Damage assessment by local, state, federal, and volunteer organizations determines losses and recovery needs.
- A major disaster declaration is requested by the governor, based on the damage assessment, and an agreement is made to commit state funds and resources to the long-term recovery.
- FEMA evaluates the request and recommends action to the White House based on the disaster, the local community, and the state's ability to recover.
- The president approves the request, or FEMA informs the governor that it has been denied. This decision process could take a few hours or several weeks depending on the nature of the disaster.

There are three major categories of disaster aid:

- Individual assistance. Immediately after the declaration, disaster workers arrive and set up a central field office to coordinate the recovery effort. A toll-free telephone number is published for use by affected residents and business owners in registering for assistance. Disaster Recovery Centers also are opened, where disaster victims can meet with program representatives and obtain information about available aid and the recovery process. Disaster aid to individuals generally falls into the following categories:
  o Disaster housing may be available for up to 18 months, using local resources, for displaced people whose residences were heavily damaged or destroyed. Funding also can be provided for housing repairs and replacement of damaged items to make homes habitable.

o Disaster grants are available to help meet other serious disaster-related needs and necessary expenses not covered by insurance and other aid programs. These may include replacement of personal property, and transportation, medical, dental, and funeral expenses.

o Low-interest disaster loans are available after a disaster for homeowners and renters from the U.S. Small Business Administration to cover uninsured property losses. Loans may be for repair or replacement of homes, automobiles, clothing, or other damaged personal property. Loans are also available to businesses for property loss and economic injury.

o Other disaster aid programs include crisis counseling, disaster-related unemployment assistance; legal aid; and assistance with income tax, social security, and veterans' benefits. Other state or local help also may be available.

o After an application is taken, the damaged property is inspected to verify the loss. If approved, an applicant will soon receive a check for rental assistance or a grant. Loan applications require more information, and approval may take several weeks after application. The deadline for most individual assistance programs is 60 days following the president's MDD.

• Public assistance. Public assistance is aid to state or local governments to pay part of the costs of rebuilding a community's damaged infrastructure. Generally, public assistance programs pay for 75 percent of the approved project costs. Public assistance may include debris removal, emergency protective measures and public services, repair of damaged public property, loans needed by communities for essential government functions, and grants for public schools.

• Hazard mitigation. Government funding can help communities avoid the life and property risks of future disasters. Examples include the elevation or relocation of chronically flood-damaged homes away from flood hazard areas; retrofitting buildings to make them resistant to earthquakes or strong winds; and adoption and enforcement of adequate codes and standards by local, state, and federal governments. FEMA helps fund damage mitigation measures.

ELIGIBILITY CRITERIA

Eligibility criteria vary depending on the nature and category of the disaster and related funding sources (federal, state, local, nongovernmental agency).

CONTACT INFORMATION

Contact FEMA, the state disaster relief agency, and the local chapter of the American Red Cross.

Useful Tips

Information is available concerning a wide range of disasters:

- Dam failure (http://www.fema.gov/hazard/damfailure/index. shtm)
- Earthquake (http://www.fema.gov/hazard/earthquake/index. shtm)
- Fire (http://www.fema.gov/hazard/fire/index.shtm)
- Flood (http://www.fema.gov/hazard/flood/index.shtm)
- Hazardous chemicals (http://www.fema.gov/hazard/chemical/ index.shtm)
- Hazardous material (http://www.fema.gov/hazard/hazmat/index. shtm)
- Heat (http://www.fema.gov/hazard/heat/index.shtm)
- Hurricane (http://www.fema.gov/hazard/hurricane/index.shtm)
- Landslide and debris flow (mudflow) (http://www.fema.gov/ hazard/landslide/index.shtm)
- Nuclear power plant emergency (http://www.fema.gov/hazard/ nuclear/index.shtm)
- Terrorism (explosions, biological threats, chemical threats, nuclear blast, radiological dispersion device) (http://www.fema.gov/ hazard/terrorism/index.shtm)
- Thunderstorm and lightning (http://www.fema.gov/hazard/ thunderstorm/index.shtm)
- Tornado (http://www.fema.gov/hazard/tornado/index.shtm)

- Tsunami (http://www.fema.gov/hazard/tsunami/index.shtm)
- Volcano (http://www.fema.gov/hazard/volcano/index.shtm)
- Wildfire (http://www.fema.gov/hazard/wildfire/index.shtm)
- Winter storm and extreme cold (http://www.fema.gov/hazard/winter/index.shtm)

Disaster relief agencies include, but are not limited to, the following:

- American Red Cross (http://www.redcross.org/)
- Federal Emergency Management Agency (FEMA) (http://www.fema.gov/)
- Salvation Army (http://www.salvationarmyusa.org/).

ABOUT THE AUTHOR

FREDERIC G. REAMER, PhD, is a professor in the graduate program of the School of Social Work, Rhode Island College. His research and teaching have addressed a wide range of human service issues, including mental health, health care, criminal justice, struggling teens, and professional ethics. Dr. Reamer has served as a social worker in correctional and mental health settings and has lectured extensively nationally and internationally on the subjects of professional ethics and professional malpractice and liability. Dr. Reamer received the Presidential Award from the National Association of Social Workers and the Distinguished Contributions to Social Work Education award from the Council on Social Work Education.

Dr. Reamer's books include *Heinous Crime: Cases, Causes, and Consequences* (Columbia University Press); *Pocket Guide to Essential Human Services* (NASW Press); *Criminal Lessons: Case Studies and Commentary on Crime and Justice* (Columbia University Press); *Social Work Values and Ethics* (Columbia University Press); *Tangled Relationships: Managing Boundary Issues in the Human Services* (Columbia University Press); *Ethical Standards in Social Work: A Review of the NASW Code of Ethics* (NASW Press); *The Social Work Ethics Audit: A Risk Management Tool* (NASW Press); *Ethics Education in Social Work* (Council on Social Work Education); *The Foundations of Social Work Knowledge* (Columbia University Press; editor and contributor); *Social Work Malpractice and Liability* (Columbia University Press); *Social Work Research and Evaluation Skills* (Columbia University Press); *The Philosophical Foundations of Social Work* (Columbia University

Press); AIDS and Ethics (Columbia University Press; editor and contributor); Ethical Dilemmas in Social Service (Columbia University Press); Rehabilitating Juvenile Justice (Columbia University Press; coauthor, Charles H. Shireman); The Teaching of Social Work Ethics (The Hastings Center; coauthor, Marcia Abramson); Finding Help for Struggling Teens: A Guide for Parents and the Professionals Who Work with Them (NASW Press; coauthor, Deborah H. Siegel); Teens in Crisis: How the Industry Serving Struggling Teens Helps and Hurts Our Kids (Columbia University Press; coauthor, Deborah H. Siegel); and The Social Work Ethics Casebook—Cases and Commentary (NASW Press).